For The Black Woman

A How-To Guide
For Developing & Elevating
The Growing & Intelligent
Sister

By
Rose Hakim

Published by Secretarius MEMPS
12685 Dorsett Rd #187 • Maryland Height, Missouri [63043]
Ph./Fax 314.564.4003
Email: secmm@sbcglobal.net
www.memps.com

First Edition
Second Edition 2005

ISBN 1-884855-57-1

Printed in the United States of America

DEDICATION

To the Followers
of
Elijah Muhammad,
Messenger of Allah,
That came at the first hour and
those at the eleventh hour.
To those who believed based on seeing and
To those who believe without seeing.

~ ~ ~ ~ ~

PREFACE

Writing an introduction for this book is surely a high honor. Never before my encounter with the teachings of Elijah Muhammad, Messenger of Allah, have I had an understanding worthy enough for consideration.

To understand the Black woman is equal to seeking an understanding of the second self of God; for until recently, we as men didn't know what she was for. We only knew that we couldn't do without her. After being taught by God's Messenger, we are beginning to understand.

In understanding my relationship and responsibilities as a husband, father, maintainer, protector and provider, I use my understanding of the relationship of Allah (God), Master Fard Muhammad and His Messenger Elijah Muhammad, as a basis for what I am about to offer to this book.

It has been some time since the black man has been in his glory. We would hear bits and pieces about it when referencing the history of the great African Songhai Empire, particularly Timbuktu and its great seat of learning.

In the days when no European had yet managed to penetrate the interior of West Africa and the horors of the Atlantic slave trade had not even been imagined, a great civilization arose along the Niger River. Established by the Songhai, a nation of black-skinned scholars, warriors, merchants, farmers, and artisans, the empire that bore their name became well known throughout North Africa, Southwest Asia, and Europe for its power and wealth.

Volumes of books are written about the causes of the black man's fall from glory. The emphasis of this books address a more sociological approach to understanding the current conditions and the trends established as a result.

It will give you a glimpse into various specific causes of the black man and woman's condition seldom explored, the cause of their division beyond the Willie Lynch Syndrome, how the conditions are perpetuated, the ugly side of it persistence and how its being divinely addressed. Yet, with it comes responsibility of our parts.

This book is designed to give you a crutch of faith in the event you have either run out or only had a little to begin with. You may not see Elijah Muhammad or the God he represents to us, but there is no star capable of shining if there is no Sun around somewhere, because stars can only reflect the light of the Sun; therefore, one could not shine without the Sun. This means that if you are still getting a little light, know that the Sun may not be seen, but it is conclusively recognized. You don't see the gravity, but you do see yourself not floating off, which tells you that gravity is still present. You are still getting Elijah's Light that he got from Master Fard Muhammad, this means there is still a source of light still around. Good manner comes from the civilized man who does not fail to perform his duty. Rose is a highly civilized woman and I am gratified to know that the sister who takes what she is imparting and improves herself, will change into a higher state of civilization as she has.

You may be an experience sister in the Nation of Islam, one who has currently started your journey back to the knowledge of self, or perhaps one who is simply testing the water before committing to reclaiming your own self and kind. Either way, there is much you can get from this book and benefit.

In today's uncertain climate, many are searching for a better way and better understanding of that way. For the new sisters, don't feel alone. Like all new brother reclaiming their own, sisters too "START" somewhere.

We all have been at this point in our development. We all had to start.

It is natural and expected for you to have questions about why did God make the woman and her origin. You will be curious about why is there a need for restoring her if you thought the woman was alright. Many sister wonder why is there so much spousal abuse in the black family and why is there so many killings involving husbands and mates. Questions concerning why the sudden increase of women killing their husbands and mates have become more frequent. Then, there are hundreds more questions the new sister doesn't know to ask. This is where this book comes in and renders help.

The black woman is made to believe that she is the last one to whom the world looks for an example of beauty, but this is all a ploy to debase here and discredit her.

Many sister come to us with very low self-esteem. We believe that God is the restorer of her and is well able to do the best job.

We are asked in scripture, "Who can find a virtuous woman? For her price is far above rubies. The heart of her husband doth safely trust in her, so that he shall have no need of spoil. She will do him good and not evil all the days of her life. She seeketh wool, and flax, and worketh willingly with her hands. She is like the merchants' ships; she bringeth her food from afar. She riseth also while it is yet night, and giveth meat to her household, and a portion to her maidens. She considereth a field, and buyeth it: with the fruit of her hands she planteth a vineyard. She girdeth her loins with strength, and strengtheneth her arms. She perceiveth that her merchandise is good: her candle goeth not out by night. She layeth her hands to the spindle, and her hands hold the distaff. She stretcheth out her hand to the poor; yea, she reacheth forth her hands to the needy. She is not afraid of the snow for her household: for all her household are clothed with scarlet. She maketh herself coverings of tapestry; her clothing is silk and purple. Her husband is known in the gates, when he sitteth among the elders of the land. She maketh fine linen, and selleth it; and delivereth girdles unto the merchant. Strength and honour are her clothing; and she shall rejoice in time to come. She openeth her mouth with wisdom; and in her tongue is the law of kindness. She looketh well to the ways of her household, and eateth not the bread of idleness. Her children arise up, and call her blessed; her husband also, and he praiseth her. Many daughters have done virtuously, but thou excellest them all. Favour is deceitful, and beauty is vain: but a woman that feareth the Lord, she shall be praised. Give her of the fruit of her hands; and let her own works praise her in the gates. Proverb: 31:10-3.

Many of you are black pearls, but simply do not know it, nor do you know how to tap the power of it with which God has equipped you.

Nasir Makr Hakim
Minister of Elijah Muhammad, Messenger of Allah

ACKNOWLEDGEMENT

And the judging on that day will be just; so as for those whose good deeds are heavy, they are the successful (H.Q. CH. 7:8)

I am very thankful to Almighty Allah (God), Master Fard Muhammad and His Last and Greatest Messenger, the Honorable Elijah Muhammad, for blessing me with enough humility and gratitude to thank those who forge the way for me.

I have learned that in most cases, once one comes into the reality of God and their place in this creation, they're willing to give up many possessions that may be very important to them to do this work; so I appreciate and know that it is their sacrifices and hard work which has helped me to become a better person.

First of all I would like to thank Sister Zanovia Jami for the being an example for me as I walked through the doors of Islam for the very first time. Her presence (dressed in full uniform) made it easier for me to accept my own and be myself. I have always admired her creativity; she is the only Sister I've known to have created and sown a family size tent. It looked like a house sitting on the camp -grounds (smile.)

Secondly, many thanks to my first Minister, Kursheed Jami, for holding his nose and putting up with my proud behavior about things I didn't understand; yet, he was kind enough to offer me the opportunity of leadership. I am thankful to Allah that Brother Kursheed allowed me to contribute something of good to the Sisterhood.

I have heard it taught that a good teacher teaches in such a way that, "In the absence of the teacher, the training will rise up and meet the occasion." This principle characterizes another important person in my development; so, thirdly and most earnestly, the Messenger trained her excellently; I speak of no other than Sister Captain Bayyinah Sharrieff Hamzah.

Of all the Muslim women I've met, who were trained and taught by Elijah Muhammad, Messenger of Allah, she is by far the best teacher of Black women in North America, by whom, I have had the privilege of being trained.

The first time I listen to her, I knew the Messenger had touched her heart and through her, he has touched mine. Many thanks for her time and the valuable lessons I've learned from her as a student.

Lastly, I want to thank my very close friend, companion and husband of many years, Minister Nasir Hakim; for his hard work and professionalism that went into the compilation of this book; also for his strong - support and humble character. He has always found joy in helping our people. Sometimes the very ones he'd help, would curse or insult him within seconds of the good deed.

Occasionally, this type of behavior would happen in my presence or others; we'd get very angry and want to defend my husband, but he would always maintain his composure. This is hard except for the humble and I commend him on his self-control. He constantly reminds me of what the Messenger said: "Unless you humble yourself, you will not see the Hereafter." This is a powerful attribute to posses and many don't know how to use it. My husband is quite intelligent and he is one of the hardest- working Black men I have ever known. His hard work and dedication to the Honorable Elijah Muhammad is undefinable; yet, he has always been there for his family and many others. Even at this late date, he's still trying to help shape me into what I'm yet to become. I have come to see that the closest I will ever get to the Honorable Elijah Muhammad, is through my husband's example. I am very thankful to Allah for him.

I pray to Allah, my sisters, that through my experiences shared in this book, you too will be able to benefit from some of the higher offerings of Islam as taught by Elijah Muhammad, Messenger of Allah.

Sister Rose Hakim
Captain, MGT/GCC
Muslim Girl Training & General Civilization Class

FROM A STUDENT TO TEACHER

A Special Thanks To The Author

Thank you Sister Captain Rose for the courage and strength that you have displayed throughout the years and for the kindness you have personally shown me.

May Allah, Master Fard Muhammad, bless you in your efforts to bring culture and dignity to Black women.

Sister Rebecca Rahman
Los Angeles, CA

TABLE OF CONTENT

The Muslim Woman goes natural. When you see her, you are looking at natural beauty.

(All Introductory Sayings are by the Honorable Elijah Muhammad, Messenger of Allah)

A THUMBNAIL OF A BEGINNING

The black woman here in North America has become the most disrespected, the most misused and the most abuse woman on the planet. She has been walked on and thrown in the mud by most cultures. She is looked upon as a servant to the world. This type of treatment has had devastating emotional impact on her. I believe that every woman wants to feel needed and respected. Every woman likes some kind of attention, to be notice by others, to feel special to someone. This natural inclination of the woman, the black woman in particular, has been exploited beyond belief.

Our exploitation goes back thousands of years. According to Elijah Muhammad, Messenger of Allah, there was a time we lived in what's now called the Middle East, and our lifestyle was consistent with nature and the laws of nature. When we started interacting with a strange new people, this is when the trouble started. We were first surreptitiously endeared to other women who were unalike in color and nature. Consequently, we befriended them and became endearing, as females are prone to do. We were taught many things by her, among these things were acts that are considered in today's world as lewd and immoral. Considering that this slow blade was being used in the dark corners of the homes, it was difficult to detect and this is one reason it flowed so easily among the righteous women. After that kind of close interaction and secrecy, the relationship had become very close. The endearing made us trust them and their word. When they began reporting information to us, we took it as truth. The fact that it was truth, but had falsehood added to it, gave us our first experience with tricknology, the science of tricks. We didn't realize that their collective approach and intent had bigger ramifications.

When they would tell us, and we in turn told our husbands, that they saw or heard something about this one or that one, we took them at their word as reliable witnesses; consequently, we believed them. After a while, we began accusing one another, based on their testimony, which resulted in brothers fighting brothers or sisters fighting sisters. This turned our Holy Land, a land that had not till that point, seen any violence and murder as we began seeing. The confusion turned our land upside down. Holy Land is being defined here as, "a place that had not been diluted, mixed or tampered with in any form."

After the Holy people would start fighting and killing one another, the white man would offer to mediate between parties and if we allowed him, he would intercede on behalf of them both to "make peace" again. This act would make the two quarreling parties endeared to him; thus, giving the man the ability to rule them both. The white man and woman have come a long way using the "divide and conquer" tactic on the original people of the planet earth.

I have covered a lot of history, the intimate details of which, many of my sisters - and brothers - don't know, but that detail I will save for our Minister to share at another time and forum.

Permit me to jump ahead and start with the period we were brought into America and the effects of chattel slavery inflicted on us by the white slave-masters, and still perpetuated crudely and scientifically by his children to this day.

CHATTEL THAT'S CONSIDERED THREE FIFTHS HUMAN

Chattel, in Law, is defined as a movable article of personal property. It also means any article of tangible property other than land, buildings, and other things annexed to land. Such could constitute equipment or livestock for example. Within this definition is where a slave fits. The American slave was considered property of an owner. The slave owner had rights to the enjoyment of the slave, as with any of the other livestock of economic value, whether the enjoyment was exclusive or shared, present or prospective. The rightful possession of such rights is called ownership. Ownership, necessarily, is supported by correlative rights to exclude others from enjoyment. By extension of usage, the things in which one has property rights are called one's property; thus the person who holds title to a slave, even though the price paid for it was still outstanding in some cases, calls it his or her "property."

What made chattel the descriptive aspect of the relationship, is that it was based on a relationship of dominance and submission, whereby one person owns another and can exact from that person labor or other services at liberty without any oversight, legal or moral.

If the above wasn't dismal enough, the white woman was being abused and discriminated against as well, but don't let me even give you the slightest notion that it was equal by no means. If it wasn't for the black woman, perhaps not one of them would have survived the sadistic, animalistic, brute like, reprobate nature of the white man. He brought all of that to us, which spared the white woman that inhumane treatment to free her up for matters like fighting for the vote.

This lilly white pursuit is what brought about the feminist movement for the political, social, and educational equality of white women with white discriminatory, unjust men. The movement has occurred mainly in Great Britain and the United States. It has its roots in the in-humanism of the 18th century and in the Industrial Revolution. Feminist issues range from access to employment, education, child-care, contraception, and abortion, to equality in the workplace, changing family roles, redress for sexual harassment in the workplace, and the need for equal political representation. Their ability to get the vote and a little equality with their man, still left the black woman, a property, suffering in ways civilized people care to forget. How did she fair?

Chattel slavery put the black man and woman on the level of beasts and livestock. Our children were sold as all other livestock, we were made to eat the worst food imaginable. We were treated worst than the other animals by virtue of being hung and burned on trees. History shows that for sport, one of the pleasures they would have with their female property, was to actually cut the unborn from the mother's womb and allow her to bleed to death right in front of them as they laughed. Another sport would be for them to bury us up to the neck with only our heads showing and allow dogs to viscously feast on it. The atrocities didn't stop there, rape was common. They had to form an American Slave Code to curtail the extent of their barbarism, because it was embarrassing their Northern brother. They were actually sexually destroying the little black girls before their organs were developed enough to bear children. They passed a code that at least made them wait until they were 12 years old. No black man was allowed to touch a virgin at all. The slave-master had to have intercourse with her first. Regardless of whether she became pregnant or not, the mulatto or half-breed would still be sold like all the other live stock. It didn't matter that the father was the white slave-master. If he would have sex with his "livestock," and I don't mean just his slave, then we have already questioned if he is human or not.

This condition rendered the black man and woman of the level of beasts, which had no need for morals, ethics and culture. If you now let them go free, what would any livestock do, but wander from pasture to pasture, looking for food and some place to sleep and procreate (have sex). This became their lifestyle. On top of this they were never educated in such a way to even know that they were humans and justified human rights. But they didn't know that they didn't know. So once freed, they were free, but only in a vacuum. It was like freeing a 7 year old. They were culturally animals, without the knowledge of themselves or anyone else.

What Good Is Freedom Without Restoration?

As a result of chattel slavery, the damage was done. To correct or reverse this most heinous crime against black people, no rehabilitative education was established to undo the unique and hidden mental stab wounds, which actually resulted in mentally killing us as a people. We are dead to our original names, language, culture, our God and our religion. We have been in a grave of ignorance since then.

The slave-master of America and the Western world lifts up the white woman as the universal symbol of beauty. We were always made to respect her, beautify her and worship her as our standard of beauty.

Today, in these modern times, we find ourselves feeling strange around other women of other nations. Why we feel this way seems to go unanswered; however, the God we intend to introduce you to has come to save us. Part of that saving is giving us a clear understanding of the causes of our unwanted and denied presence in the better moral and more cultured societies. No civilized people want to be in the presence of people who act like animals, whether they act that way intentionally or not. As a direct result of the intentional destruction of the Black man and woman's civilizing properties, not only were the slaves prone to act like the chattel they were conditioned to be, but they will unknowingly teach it to all forthcoming generations.

The civilized world don't look at it as they should. They only see it from the surface; consequently, they reject us because the white race rejects us. This is why the scriptures refer to us as the rejected and the despised. This general condition makes us hungry for acceptance, but we are the only ones who don't know that we don't know. In other words, we are not aware of the serious damage that's been done to us. Consequently, we think that we are alright and just like everybody else. Therefore, my sisters, when you try interacting in certain circles, something always seem to be a little off color or "strange." This starts setting up a state of denial and it shows in our faces.

This does not only effect our beautiful facial expression, but throws the mental power of many black women into confusion and from this comes the unwelcome words: **"I DO NOT CARE HOW I LOOK" or "WHAT I DO IS NO ONES BUSINESS BUT MY OWN**." Consequently, such a one becomes another unfit mother to suckle and train our oncoming generation, gone to the dogs of humanity. I must qualify what I am about to say, because there will be those among you who may be offended; however, truth is known to hurt the guilty. Yet, as Jesus taught, it will also free you.

Almighty Allah, Master Fard Muhammad, through His Messenger, Elijah Muhammad, taught us that the Black Woman is completely robbed of the knowledge of herself. She weighs other than herself. The white slave-master taught her to eat the wrong food and to eat it three times a day, and in between meals. He teaches her to drink strong beverages, and make herself fat like a poison animal. She in turn becomes shapeless, ugly, kinked hair, ignorant, and degraded to the extent that no one of high morals would want such a woman or girl. The overweight causes her to suffer from rheumatism, headaches, pains in all joints, and she soon becomes lazy, careless, hopeless, using snuff and tobacco. When she stops caring about herself, she starts wearing filthy clothes, sitting in her filthy room or house, and sleeping all during the day and night.

She quarrels at all times with her family, and uses the most ugly and dirty language at home or in public. If chastised by the better society, she accuses them of not being any better than she is, or not as good as she is. She hates the intelligent sisters of her neighborhood; she sits in her door or at her window and watch for all men, to offer her body. She loves and enjoys all men, except her husband. She unknowingly helps to uphold her own sons and daughters in acts of adultery.

If her husband's friends visit him, she stops all her housework to sit in their presence, or in an adjoining room where she can catch the eye of her husband's friend. If he is not affected by her alluring acts, she does not like him. She is full of lies, and always working to deceive her husband. She hates to take baths, but only once a week. Then she takes a total ablution. She carries a very foul odor, and fears the bathtub when in regular menstruation period; then she takes cold and causes the flow to stop.

She always buys her shoes too small and with a high cork heel. This causes corns on her toes and causes her anklebone to (grow inward). Many times she pulls off her shoes in the presence of company.

She moves real slow and watches everybody, to see if she is being noticed. She buys all the rubbing medicine and headache pills, laxatives, which the slave-master manufactures. Now she sits down overweighed, with fat and aching limbs, high blood pressure and waits for death. This is a sad and miserable condition, in which this slave-master has the earth's most beautiful woman.

Half of her children are sometimes bastard children. They marry, and if not pregnant by their husbands soon as expected, he is labeled as no good; then she slips out and gets children by another man, and accuses them of being her husbands children, to cover her adulteress acts. This is a sad picture of our sisters living in the wilderness of North America. They have been made so unclean.

Recent surveys by several Asiatic nurses have shown that only one girl out of every 700 is a virgin. A Harlem Hospital in New York City proves this. There, the record showed that this number is being taken from schoolgirls, and that there are girls being caught giving birth to babies in school toilets. And school teachers are many times the fathers and mothers of these indecent acts of adultery.

As a result of this horrible condition and the wide distribution of videos and movies depicting us as savage and prostitutes, many foreign people come to America already assuming that we are lower than human.

Our sisters who are living such a life, have the pains of rejection at the door of every intelligent society. They try to join themselves to the intelligent Black Asiatic young men, and even the slave-master bars them in matrimony. They are only recognized at the back door in the dark, as prostitutes. Likewise, they are denied high paying positions in society. Their presence is frowned upon at dinner tables and dancing parties given by moral societies. No well-refined and perfect-formed woman or girl will class with such overweight, undeveloped, indecent, lazy, careless, ugly and over average breather.

Our homes are destroyed by home breakers, children destroyers, sick, diseased, unbridled tongues, husband deceivers, and lovers of strange men. This is why we are rejected and our company shunned.

The Black Woman is always disappointed; consequently, she becomes troubled and agitated very often. Her life is generally depressed and easily enraged. Her feelings and emotions run high which are abnormal. She eventually goes insane and loses all hope of moral respect from intelligent society. She eventually begins destroying her life by trying to co-habitate or mixes the blood of many men in her womb at the same time.

It becomes what she thinks is, "natural" to eat poison food, go unclean, and ignorant of how to be a healthy pregnant mother. Consequently, this potential mother dies at the change of life, the age of 47. Few children are born to the lost-found mother after this age.

My dear black sisters, you have fallen so far from the right way, that now you are no more admired, but are looked upon as most hateful. Many higher classed women whisper among themselves saying: **"ARE THESE THE NOBELS THAT WERE TO BE FOR THE LOST FOUNDS? NOW THEY HAVE DEGRADED THEMSELVES."**

We are asked by God…

"You have fallen, gone back to that which your Saviour came and pulled you out. What meaning have you in painting your faces, putting false eyebrows on, reddening your nails, painting your lips and cheeks. Your hair is burned out from straightening by hot irons and using the swine grease on it and on thine faces. You are dressing in tight form fitting clothes, so as to show thy form and thus tempt men and boys to commit adultery with thee.

You have gone and stood in highways and on the street corners and winked thine eyes. Yea: and opened thine feet to strangers to whosoever will. Yea: You are like a red-hot oven, the filthy lust of adultery is eating you up. You have brought shame upon your Nation, as well as your family. Your innocent children, your husbands cannot hold their heads up before the Nations, because of your lewd ways of adultery. You have loved the ways of the white race and despised your own in which our Saviour, Master Fard Muhammad, has brought thee. The cry of adultery is in the city, throughout the country, from women and girls, for men to come and lie with them that their shame may be increased."

In several of the larger cities, our women and virgin daughters are hiring out themselves to the slave-master to use their bodies for fornication. These evil adulteresses are sometimes found among the so-called society spreading untold misery of the white man's disease, besides corrupting their children with such diseases as Whites and Syphilis.

Where are we to rise from such a shameful generation, following after the style of the white race? We have thrown our intelligence into the garbage can. Our little children going to the white man's schools and sweet-hearting with little white boys and girls. This starts them inclining to adultery, and vice of all kinds. Know you not that 90% of our girl virgins are destroyed by whites? And nearly the same percentage is corrupting our homes between man and wife. This started from the white insurance agents, our women working in the white's homes and offices.

Nurses are attacked by white men and are lured by a few shiny nickels, or for steady employment. You have fallen, but your Saviour and mine has come to save us and who the Saviour is will be taught in depth by the Minister, in another book titled, The True History of Master Fard Muhammad.

All of the blame doesn't fall on us my sisters; however, you must understand our condition. This helps you to see why we need a Saviour, because if many of our sisters could get out of the terrible condition they are in, by themselves, don't you think they and we would have done so by now? We need a Saviour.

We have been blinded to our greatness and force fed the image of the white woman from infancy to old age, but did you know that the white woman has been and is today one the worse sources of evil you will find in a human. I stated at the beginning of this chapter, it was her who showed us all the lewd ways we now practice.

In the teachings of the Honorable Elijah Muhammad, we're taught that when the father of the white race Yakub, taught them how to deceive the black man, he taught them to go and rent rooms among them, and it was actually the white woman who rented the rooms. After doing so, the white woman introduced lesbianism to the Black woman. She taught the Black woman various lewd acts, positions and tricks. Having learned all of these new techniques, the black woman in turn would try using them on her husband, and he would question her about their origin, (you know, where did you learn that) considering she had never done this to him before, but the nature of his righteous mind would not allow him to go very far in questioning her about it.

This skillful and wickedly wise positioning of the white woman, among the black women, created the type of bonding that, when the white woman would tell the black woman that she saw this or that, (you know, girl I saw your best friend with your husband last night) then the Black woman would take it as the truth, because of the level of endearment between and her new intimate friend. So, seeing that the black woman trusted her, the white woman began creating confusion by putting brother against brother, sister against sister, household against household, and it was at this point that her man, the white man, would step in to help settle their differences, and if they permitted him to, then he ruled both households (the black man and black woman).

So today, after the white man has virtually destroyed the Black man's connection with his God, destroyed his ability to be a maintainer, provider and protector, of his Black woman, the white slave-master has rendered the black man on the level of a beast or has neutralized him as a man, which in turn leaves the white MAN, as the only MAN, who has power over the black woman, and the black man as the widow's son.

The black man was killed mentally and the black woman was left a widow who has been protecting her sons since slavery time, just like a conquering male lion will kill all the cubs of a previous litter and take over the clan of female lions. If she doesn't submit, the male will kill her too. Today, most of the men that has come through slavery have the white man's name, religion, mentality and immorality. Coupled with those characteristics is the fact that the black man was used as a Stud or bull to produce kids, which is the name for animal offspring, versus children to people, for the master's economic prowess.

There is an account of a slave revolt that took place in Virginia. It consisted of two studs being sent out to fight one another. The two slave owners wanted a monopoly on slave sales. Both owners had lots of slaves; yet, they were fierce competitors.

When Gabriel Prosser and Black Jack Bowler met that night, instead of them fighting, they united and organized one the biggest slave insurrection in Virginia's history. Before their insurrection was eventually stopped, between the two of them, they had sired a little under 1200 children for the slave trading economy.

As a result of these immoral practices and conditions, the black man, like the woman, was let loose without any civilizing restoration, without any ethics, without any morals, without any hope and without any guide other than what they had learned as chattel. In their effort to act according to what they learned as being civil, they began treating their woman as bad as the white man.

ABUSE: ALL IN THE FAMILY

Today, many of us are being sexually abused, exploited or misused by our OWN men, and have resorted to finding comfort from our sisters. Unfortunately, in many cases, it leads to extremes, because of a lack of morals or poor scruples. This is only compounded in a filthy world as the Western world, which promotes the most bizarre sexual behavior from sex gadgets to animalism; consequently, many of our sisters are spiritually as well as mentally destroyed. As a result of doing what the white woman does, when the Black woman is destroyed, our whole nation is destroyed too. Now, by us not knowing the whole story or all the dynamics of the whole story of what has happen to us and our men, it leaves us all, black man and woman, with trying to figure out what's happening to us within the limited scope of our understanding. We only see the surface of his abuse on us, and we only see the surface of our abuse on him. We both are allowed to think that problem is between us and on the surface it is; yet, to understand the deep psychological, mental and spiritual scars we carry, we must go to the root if we truly want to treat our unique condition. We find ourselves seeing the situation statistically instead of historically. The expression or the degree of our destruction is played out in our lifestyle.

Let's look at some of the external aspects of destruction, which comes to us from our frustrated and disconnected sons who grow up physically as men, are still spiritually, mentally, socially, economically and politically bankrupt:

It takes the following forms:

- Verbal abuse
- Physical abuse
- Death

Like us, our men constantly measure us up against the white woman, because, like us, she has become the standard of beauty among all women. Many men result to verbal abuse in the initial form of sarcasm or sly insults when they believe you are not living up to that standard. If they buy you gifts, it has that intent, because they too are trying to compete with other men to see whose woman can look like the white woman the most.

Being in the position as the black man, being stripped of the power to be the man over his family, community and nation, he is rendered powerless and this is the last position he needs to be in if he wants to have the respect and honor of his women and children. Although there is a super show of deception going on in America, attempting to convince the once slaves that they are free, reality just won't go away. Our very nature tells us that we are not. In a subtle condition of making it difficult for the black man to get a decent education or job to support his family, he has been rendered incapable to maintain a family. Second to this is the easy educating and hiring of the woman, it simultaneously and cleverly transforms her into the household bread winner; thus displacing most black households. What's not published is the fact that it is not the nature of a man to submit in this fashion to his woman, and still believe he is a man. This unsaid status frustrates most men and this frustration, if not understood by us my sisters, which is generally the case, result in explosive domestic violence. We then end up calling the MAN, as we use to call the police, to come arrest our BOY-friend and take him out of our CRIB.

Women Killed By Husbands or Partners

Domestic Violence Statistics

According to FBI statistics, 30% of female murder victims in 1990, the last year for which statistics are available, were killed by their husbands or boyfriends. That is approximately 3000 women. *(Caroline Knapp, "A Plague of Murders: Open Season on Women, The Boston Phoenix, August 1992)*

In 1990, says the FBI, intimate enemies accounted for 30% of all women murder victims *("Doctors must join fight against domestic violence," USA Today, June 18, 1992, at 12-A)*

According to the Uniform Crime Report of the Federal Bureau of Investigation, 30% of women killed in the United States die at the hands of a husband or boyfriend. In 1990, more than 800 women were killed by their husbands; 400 more were killed by their boyfriends. *(Antonia C. Novello, "From the Surgeon General, U.S. Public Health Service, A Medical Response to Domestic Violence," Journal of the American Medial Association, June 17, 1992, p. 3132)*

One-third of all female homicide victims are killed by husbands, ex-husbands, boyfriends or ex-boyfriends. (NCJA Justice Research, "States, Federal Government

Increasing Focus on Violence Against Women."
September/October 1990, p. 3)

More than twice as many women are killed by their husbands or boyfriends as are murdered by strangers. *(Arthur Kellerman, "Men, Women and Murder," The Journal of Trauma, July 17, 1992, pp. 1-5)*

In a study of females killed by intimate partners between 1980-1982, it was found that the majority of women killed were married *(57.7%, n=2,415).*

Girlfriends were the next highest percentage (24.5%, n-1,041), followed by common-law wives *8%, n-332), ex-wives (4.89%, n-205) and *friends (4.675, n-196). (Karen Stout, "Intimate Femicide: A National Demographic Overview," Violence Update, Vol. 1, No. 6, February 1991, p. 3)*

More than 90 women were murdered every week in 1991 - 9 out of 10 were murdered by men. *(Violence Against Women, A Majority Staff Report, Committee on the Judiciary, United States Senate, 102nd Congress, October 1992, p. 2)*

Of the 5,745 women murdered in 1991, 6 out of 10 were killed by someone they knew. Half were murdered by a spouse or someone with whom they had been intimate. *("When Violence Hits Home," Time, July 4, 1994)*

Among all female victims in 1992, 29% were slain by boyfriends or husbands and 4% of male victims were slain by their wives or girlfriends. *(Federal Bureau of Investigations, 1993)*

Many of the stats in this section come from the National Clearinghouse for the Defense of Battered Women. National Clearinghouse for the Defense of Battered Women, 125 S. 9th Street, Suite 302, Philadelphia, PA 19107.

THE BLAME GAME

After the majority have finished their abuse, they say, ***"LOOK AT WHAT YOU MADE ME DO."*** Even in this, most will not take responsibility. This lack of responsibility almost always takes the following form of mistreatment.

He Doesn't Provide For His Woman As He Should. He Doesn't Protect Her As He Should. He Doesn't maintain her As He Should. Before you write him off as a complete dog, or he writes you off as the same, thus giving our enemies one more victory, remember, we both have been damaged, without any school of restoration addressing our unique condition of being left for dead as fetuses without our umbilical cords cut.

Since he has no knowledge of himself, how then can he know or understand the value of his woman? Therefore, she is made to feel worthless. Their relationship is largely based on primal or base habit such as eating, sex, child bearing, and materialism.

Our basic instincts have been affected by our social orientation, in that it was considered taboo to fight back; however, times have changed. We are no longer willing to stay in an abusive relationship. They are either leaving or killing the abuser.

BATTERED WOMEN WHO KILL

When women kill - and they do so at astonishingly lower rates than men who commit 85% of all homicides - the vast majority kill family members, usually men who have battered them for years. As many as 90% of the women in jail today for killing men had been battered by those men. *(Allison Bass, "Women far less likely to kill than men; no one sure why," The Boston Globe, February 24, 1992, p. 27)*

Within motive categories, male offenders dominated in murders motivated by possessiveness (m=82%), abuse (m=75%), and arguments (m=63%), whereas females were the vast majority of offenders in the category of self-defense (f=83%). By comparison, among victims whose deaths were motivated by possessiveness females comprised 59% and males 41% of the total. Similarly, among victims killed because of arguments females represented 56% and males 44% of the total. For victims of abuse, though, females were 75% of the total, while victims of self-defense were 96% male. *(from a study of 155 mate homicides in City of Jacksonville, Florida, 1980-1986). (Christine E. Rasche, "'Given' Reasons for Violence in Intimate Relationships," Homicide: The Victim/Offender*

Connection, ed. Anna Wilson (Cincinnati, OH: Anderson, 1993) p. 88)

In Jurik and Winn's study of gender and homicide, 44% (22) of the women said that a precipitating event was partner conflict compared with 8% (9) of the men.

Given this information, it is not surprising that a significantly greater percentage of women who killed stated that they acted in self-defense - 42% of the women versus 30% of the men. *(Nancy Jurik and Russ Winn, "Gender and Homicide: A Comparison of Men and Women Who Kill," Violence and Victims, Vol. 5, No. 4, 1990, p. 236)*

A study conducted in Georgia of 226 (96%) of the 235 female inmates currently serving for homicide revealed the presence of domestic violence in more than half of the cases when the woman has killed her significant other, there is some record of a history of domestic abuse. In 60% of the cases where a woman killed her significant other, the woman claims the victim assaulted or abused her at the time of the crime. *(Judith Haley, "A Study of Women Imprisoned for Homicide," Georgia Department of Corrections, June 1992, p. 16)*

According to data release in 1992 by the Georgia Department of Corrections, of the 235 women doing time for murder or manslaughter in Georgia, 44% killed a husband or lover. *(J.O. Hansen, "Is Justice Taking a Beating?" The Atlanta Constitution, April 26, 1992, A1-A7)*

Of these murders, 102 were classified as domestic killings. Forty-six women (almost half) claim that their partners beat them regularly, and 38 of these 46 had repeatedly reported domestic violence to the police. *(Kathleen O'Shea, "Women on Death Row," Women Prisoners: A Forgotten Population, Beverly Fletcher, Lynda Dixon Shaver, and Dreama Moon, eds., (Westport, CT: Praeger, 1993) p. 85)*

Currently there are 2,000 battered women in America who are serving prison time for defending their lives against their batterers. *(Stacey Kabat, Remarks from presentation at Harvard School of Public Health, Center for Health Communication, June 1991)*

Women commit 17% of all homicides and a high percentage are committed in big cities such as Houston and Philadelphia. The fear, rage, and entrapment associated with abuse can lead a woman to strike out against her assailant for sheer survival. Unfortunately, killing is often a woman's safest alternative given the absence of police protection or its ineffectiveness due to state laws requiring injury in a "domestic" before an arrest is mandated. *(Evan Stark, "Rethinking Homicide: violence, Race, and the Politics of Gender," International Journal of Health and Services, vol. 20, No. 1, 1990, p. 18)*

Four out of five victims of intimate offender resisted the assault. They passively resisted trying to get help, threatening or arguing, or using evasive action - twice as often as they actively resisted - using a weapon or fighting back. *(Caroline Harlow, Bureau of Justice Statistics, "Female Victims of Violent Crime," Washington, DC: U.S. Department of Justice, 1991, p. 6)*

In a study of 155 mate homicides in City of Jacksonville, Florida, 1980-1986, at least seven of the 24 offenders who claimed that their actions were in self-defense were prosecuted by the state, and six of them were found guilty (one was found not guilty by reason of insanity). *(Christine E. Rasche, "'Given' Reasons for Violence in Intimate Relationships," Homicide: The Victim/Offender Connection, ed. Anna Wilson (Cincinnati, OH: Anderson, 1993) p. 88)*

Among mate homicides motivated by possessiveness, there were about equal numbers of cases with verbal versus physical provocation, but for 58% of these cases there was no victim provocation at all. The absence of provocation was notable also for cases motivated by abuse (67% of which were unprovoked) and other reasons (68% unprovoked). For cases motivated by arguments, however, 44% involved physical or other provocation and another 25% had verbal provocations.

Not surprisingly, for homicides motivated by self-defense, 71% entailed physical provocations by the victim, with another 25% having verbal provocations (including threats to kill). Only 4% of claimed self-defense cases involved no apparent provocation at all. (from a study of 155 mate homicides in City of Jacksonville, Florida, 1980-1986) (Christine E. Rasche, "'Given' Reasons for Violence in Intimate Relationships," Homicide: The Victim/Offender Connection, ed. Anna Wilson *(Cincinnati, OH: Anderson, 1993) p. 95)*

In a study of 155 mate homicides in City of Jacksonville, Florida, 1980-1986, over half (56%) of these offenders either called the police themselves, confessed to the police, or both. Offenders who killed their victims in self-defense were the most likely to come forward (86%)), followed by those who killed as a result of abuse (75%), argument (66%), or for other reasons (61%). *(Christine E. Rasche, "'Given' Reasons for Violence in Intimate Relationships," Homicide: The Victim/Offender Connection, ed. Anna Wilson (Cincinnati, OH: Anderson, 1993) p. 898)*

Although women comprise more than half of the U.S. population and 23% of all homicide victims, they committed only 14.7% of the homicides reported during the study (male/female ratio = 6.33). In contrast to men, who killed nonintimate acquaintances, strangers, or individuals of undetermined relationship in roughly 80% of cases, women killed their spouse in 31.4% of cases, an intimate
acquaintance in 13.6% or a member of their family in 14.8% of cases. *(Arthur Kellerman, "Men, Women and Murder," The Journal of Trauma, July 17, 1992, p. 2)* *Most of the women in prison for homicide had only one victim (95%).* The 226 women killed 239 victims, generally their male significant other (117).

Fifty;-three percent of the women killed their significant other. The significant other category comprises legal spouse, common-law spouse, lover and ex-spouse/lover. When the women killed a significant other, they generally admitted committing the crime (82%). *(Judith Haley, "A Study of Women Imprisoned for Homicide," Georgia Department of Corrections, June 1992, p. 15)*

In 1992, the American Medical Association reported that as many as 1 in 3 women will be assaulted by a domestic partner in her lifetime - 4 million in any given year. *("When Violence Hits Home," Time, July 4, 1994)*

The average prison sentence of men who kill their women partners is 2 to 6 years. Women who kill their partners are sentenced on average to 15 years, despite the fact that most women who kill do so in self-defense *(National Coalition Against Domestic Violence, 1989).*

In two studies of homicide cases involving women who killed their partners, 75% and 44% of the women had been physically abused by them prior to the lethal incident. [Daniel and Harris (1982) in a pretrial study of women charged with homicide in Missouri] (Angela Browne and Kirk R. Williams, "Exploring the Effect of Resource Availability and the Likelihood of Female-Perpetrated Homicides," Law & Society Review, Vol. 23, No. 1, 1989, p.77), [In a study comparing the links between gender and homicide, 108 cases using data from court recorded presentence investigative resources were analyzed.] *(Nancy Jurik and Russ Winn, "Gender and Homicide: A Comparison of Men and Women Who Kill, " Voices and Victims, Vol. 5, No. 4, 1990, p. 234).*

Many of the stats in this section come from the National Clearinghouse for the Defense of Battered Women. National Clearinghouse for the Defense of Battered Women 125 S. 9th Street Suite 302 Philadelphia, PA 19107

QUESTIONS FOR THE WIDE AWAKE BLACK WOMAN

The condition we suffer can be discussed in several ways; however I am going to focus on us, my sisters, not because I hold any malice against my brothers, but because I want to stay consistent with the title of my book (smile).

Since being "freed" from slavery, the value of Black life has not been given any priority, consequently, there has been no investment in our inner development, other than the slave-master's religion, which keeps us believing that the finer things in life we won't get until after we die; although, the white man and the preacher seems to be enjoying theirs now while they are living. This brings me to some other questions:

- ✓ Why are we called African-Americans & Negroes?
- ✓ Why are we spiritually deaf, dumb and blind?
- ✓ Why is everybody making progress; yet, we seem to be lagging so far behind?
- ✓ Why are we still being mistreated?
- ✓ Why are we in this condition: Stripped of our names, our language, our culture,
  - our country, our God and our religion.

Here in America, all of our knowledge about religion and theology has come from preachers who have been groomed by the slave-master. He has told us of a heaven way up in the sky that we can't enjoy now but rather after we die; yet, all of the years that we are living, for us there is nothing but hell, pain, torture and misgiving. What's puzzling though, is that the Bible speaks of a heaven filled with material luxury, which the white man and the preacher has and enjoys right here - so we see.

There are many things I intend to share with you, but I must take you up step by step, so you will understand and enjoy what's in store for you, but in the meantime, my sisters, take it for what it's worth, heaven and hell are just two conditions of life and they both are right here on this earth.

Before we move forward, let's summarize and check back into history, which rewards our research and tells us plainly, that before the white man gained entry to the East, he was living in the caves of Europe on level of the beast. He was eating the bark of trees and eating flesh raw, until God sent Moses to civilize him and teach him the law.

Then, following many of his explorers, he gained entry into Asia and Africa. From China he took silk and gun-powder. From India he took jute, manganese and rubber. He raped Africa of her diamonds and her gold, and from the Mid-East he took barrels of oil untold. Deceiving, raping, robbing and murdering everything in his path, the whole Black World have tasted of the white man's wrath.

Before we, the Black man and woman, were brought to America, as mentioned earlier, we were living in the East by the Nile River, living in luxury, enjoying freedom, justice and equality. We wore silken robes and slippers of gold. We were the wealthiest and wisest people untold, now we are the poorest of the poor, nobody wants us at their door.

When the white man came to America, he told the Indian, "I am your white brother." The Red man took him in, taught him his best; yet, he pushed the Indian further west. With his white woman and fire water, tricks and lies, he stole America. The original owners of this nation is cooped up on a reservation.

He then needed someone to work the land, his back was too weak, he needed you and your Black man. So he commissioned Sir John Hawkins, an English slave trader, to commit the world's most grievous sin: To take a man and woman who were born to be free and bring them down to slavery and sell them as merchandise, on their bodies he put a price.

John Hawkins showed up in our country telling us of a land filled with luxury, he said Black man follow me to America, there you will find more gold for your labor. Our fore-parents were tricked onto his boat, since that time we have been wrestling with the goat. We landed here in Jamestown Virginia, 400 years to suffer.

When our slave-masters wanted to have some sport, he would heap cruelties of our parents of the worse sort: burn them at stakes, hang them on trees. His ears were deaf to our parent's pleas.

Though you were pregnant my sisters, you pulled the plow, like a horse, like a mule, sweat from your brow. He filled our wombs with his wicked seed, and like the other livestock, his half white children you were made to breed.

Yet, in our souls, hearts and eternal mind's eye, as reflected in the old Negro spirituals, we knew we belonged to someone. We would sing, "Come by here Lord, come by here." Once we were allowed to read, through the falsehood we read in the 15th chapter, verse 13 of the Bible, Genesis it read,

“And God said to Abram, know of a surety that thy seed shall be a stranger in a land that is not theirs. And they serve them and they shall afflict them 400 years, but after that time I will come and I will judge that nation which they shall serve."

We were taught by the slave-master and his indoctrinators that slavery started in the country in 1619; yet, we have learned that the first slave is recorded to have come to this country in 1555 by Sir John Hawkins of England. If you subtract the time in between 1555 and 1619, that comes to 64 years. What happened to this "forgotten time?"

THE REAL $64,000 DOLLAR QUESTION

For thousands of years, the people who did not have the knowledge of the Person or reality of God, worshipped their own ideas of God. Consequently, most know God and believe Him to be a spirit or a mystery; therefore, how could one teach about that which they themselves do not know. This point is raised, because when we read scripture, we see in many instances where God has made agreements or covenants with the peoples. Within those agreements was a price if they were true and a price if they violated their end. The scripture has always beard out that God never failed in his promise; therefore, if the Jews, like others before them are dealt with according to the same terms and they violated their part of the covenant, should we expect less from the God who never fails in His promise?

If we examine the promise made to Abraham by God concerning Abraham's seed, we would have to turn our attention to Genesis 15:13-15, wherein it reads,

"And he said unto Abram, Know of a surety that thy seed shall be a stranger in a land that is not theirs, and shall serve them; and they shall afflict them four hundred years; And also that nation, whom they shall serve, will I judge: and afterward shall they come out with great substance. And thy shalt go to thy fathers in peace; thou shalt be buried in a good old age."

We see in the Bible, St. John 8 chapter, wherein Jesus was talking to the Jews when he said,

"And ye shall know the truth, and the truth shall make you free." This statement drew a question from the Jews: "...We be Abraham's seed, and were never in bondage to any man: how sayest thou, Ye shall be made free?

Here we see that the Jews apparently didn't realize why Jesus was talking that "ole freedom talk" to them. And interestingly, if the Jews were Abraham's seed and were never in bondage to any man, who was it then, that was in bondage in the history of Moses, supposedly in Egypt? There are no Egyptian records, nor any others, which supports the enslavement of a people for 400 years other than those of America, and the so-called Negroes, were slaves in America since 1555.

This leads us into the genealogy question regarding whose father is whose. Such is taken up by Jesus and the Jews themselves further on in the book of St. John, the 8th Chapter, 38th verse, when Jesus said, "I speak that which I have seen with my Father: and ye do that which ye have seen with your father."

Here we are dealing with two different fathers! Jesus went on to use logical proofs to justify what he was saying in these verses: (39, 40) "If ye were Abraham's children, ye would do the works of Abraham. But now ye seek to kill me, a man that hath told you the truth, which I have heard of God: this did not Abraham."

It wasn't that Jesus didn't know who they were, he just didn't want to reveal it to them then; however, he apparently felt compelled when he told them, "Ye are of your father the devil, and the lust of your father ye will do. He was a murderer from the beginning, and abode not in the truth, because there is no truth in him. When he speaketh a lie, he speaketh of his own: for he is a liar and the father of it." (8:44).

The Bible, Matthew 1:21 prophesied that Jesus would be born "to save his people." If Jesus were a Jew or even the King of the Jews, (according to previous scripture) he would be referring to himself as a devil; additionally, Jesus makes a clear distinction between his father the father of the Jews. It is easy to see that the Jews were not Jesus' people.

There is a Jesus born to save his people from their sins, but those weren't his people. That Jesus of 2000 years ago wasn't the one who was to be preaching those words of resurrection. Resurrection didn't happen at that time anyway. It forces us to re-think, re-examine and agree on how Paul seen Jesus as a man before his time, and how a future Jesus was prophesied to come, even by Jesus himself.

Who could that someone be today, needing to be saved from living a life of sin, because they know no other life or even themselves? Who are these people needing to be saved from "themselves" as a result of being robbed of the natural right to know themselves? Who are a people who don't know that they do not know themselves, as a result of being displaced from their original land, names, language, culture, God and religion? Who are this people rendered on a dead level needing to be resurrected from a mental grave of ignorance? They are none other than the American so-called Negroes. They're called Negroes, because in most highly learned circles of the whites, they know they are mentally dead and they should know, because they killed them. This story about Hiram, equipped with it's ending, is symbolically acted out in the secret society of Shriners, the keepers of the dead, who know that it wasn't actually Solomon who raised him, but actually God, Himself, who was prophesied to come after the workings of Satan.

The wise know, that the fact you see Blacks in America no longer wearing slave names, and having names like Muhammad, Hakim, Karriem, Abdul, and Ali; Our Saviour Has Arrived to "save his people from their sins - practicing the ways of their enemies." It fits none other than the American so-called Negroes who have been lost in a strange land for over 400 years.
There are other questions which will eventually have to be addressed; for example, if the so-called Negroes are the "real sheep" that's been lost 400 years, and are that chosen people to be saved as prophesied by a modern day Jesus, then has there been anyone in modern times pointing out the white race's false claim to divinity as Jesus did 2000 years ago?

The nature of the two peoples, Black and White, are different. We have two different fathers, and if you think what I'm saying is harsh, then the Bibles, Romans 3:9-18 states,

"What then? Are we better than they? No, in no wise: for we have before proved both Jews and Gentiles, that they are all under sin: As it is written, There is none righteous, no, not one: There is none that understandeth, there is none that seeketh God. They are all gone out of the way, they are together become unprofitable; there is none that doeth good, no, not one. Their throat is an open sepulchre; with their tongues they have used deceit; the poison of asps is under their lips: Whose mouth is full of cursing and bitterness: Their feet are swift to shed blood; Destruction and misery are in their ways: And the way of peace have they not known: There is no God before their eyes."

What you must now know my sisters, God never fails in his promise as before mentioned and proven; we should not be surprised to see constant fulfillment in these times as well. The future Jesus has sought out the "Lost Sheep (Nation) to save them from their sins (living contrary to God's law as a result of being raised and conditioned by those contrary). His coming and raising or Resurrecting a MENTALLY dead people from the grave of ignorance, who were robbed of the knowledge of themselves and consequently thought they were rightly guided; yet they had been forced to make a living in the muck and mire of another people and nation, thinking its freedom and godly. Now, today, a marvelous light has come: God Himself, in the Person of Master Fard Muhammad, and He has raised one from among the Mentally dead as His first born raised from the Mentally dead, that one being Allah

(God's) Last and Greatest Messenger, the Honorable Elijah Muhammad.

According to Allah, Master Fard Muhammad's Last Messenger, the Most Honorable Elijah Muhammad, "Israel was not a Jew. Israel was not a Christian. Abraham was not a Jew, nor a Christian. And the Holy Qur'an teaches us that. And if you study Abraham's history, you can easily see and understand that he was not a Jew, nor was he a Christian, because Christianity had not been organized in Abraham's time.

"Christianity was just organized after the death of Jesus. Therefore, Abraham living even before Moses, could not have been his religion (Christianity), nor could he be a Jew, when there were no Jews in Abraham's time.

"There were white people, but there were no Jews. They were there in the hills and cave sides of Europe, not making any history for themselves until the birth of Moses. The white race's history begins with Moses. They count or record their history from this time." (Messenger Elijah Muhammad, The Tribe of Shabazz, 1962).

"Behold, I will make them of the synagogue of Satan, which say they are Jews, and are not, but do lie; behold, I will make them to come and worship before thy feet, and to know that I have loved thee." (Revelations 3:9)

My beautiful Black sisters, our God and Saviour Allah, Master Fard Muhammad, has come. He has declared that the white man's day is done. He has raised from us a Divine Messenger, one prophesied to come, his name is Elijah (read Bible, Malachi 4:5-6) It reads:

"Behold, I will send you Elijah the prophet before the coming of the great and dreadful day of the Lord: And he shall turn the hearts of the fathers to the children, and the hearts of the children to their fathers, lest I come and smite the earth with a curse."

Selected Writings By Request

I have had the privilege of writing to address the needs of my sisters for over ten years. Although many of my brothers have written to me and expressed a great appreciation for the articles, many of my sisters were able to benefit even more. I am grateful to my sisters who were able to apply what they have read and as a result, improved their lives. That improvement is payment enough for me, because so often, we find ourselves not benefiting from the experience of those who went before us. Consequently, we find ourselves reinventing the wheel over and over. This occurs, because we never pass on the benefit of our learning to the generations after us. In an extreme case, we die with the knowledge still in our heads not knowing that we kill part of our future when we do that.

In an earnest effort to do my part, I have collected and compiled the articles, which were most requested, and put them in this book. I pray to Allah, that they help those who can benefit.

WE MUST BE CIVILIZED WITH GOD'S WISDOM - FIRST!

We cannot change ourselves unless we change our way of thinking. It is actually thought that changes us.

Why do we need a new civilization? What's wrong with the one we have? The duty of a civilized man is to teach civilization, the arts and sciences of civilized people to the uncivilized.

As black women living here in the hells of North America, we must ask ourselves this question, in our present condition, have we been properly civilized, and if so, who's standards are we using as a measuring tool?

Before we try to answer that question, let's understand what civilization actually is. As Webster defines it, "Civilization is the condition of being civilized; social organization of high standard, marked by advances in the arts, sciences, etc." It is the total culture of a people, nation and period. It is the countries and people considered to have reached a high stage of cultural development.

To civilize means to teach the Wisdom and Knowledge of the human family of the planet earth, or to bring out of a condition of savagery to instruct in the ways of an advanced society, to teach people how to live a useful and unsavage life.

So, to answer the above question, yes we need a new civilization, because the slave master has failed to perform his duty of civilizing the so-called American Negro in America, and it has left many of us in a savage state of mind. Those of us who follow the teachings of the Honorable Elijah Muhammad, has and is being guided out of this savage state by learning and being re-educated in the following ways:

1. We must learn about our own black people and have a knowledge of self, others, sciences and God, in this world - and to act on the basis of that knowledge; for with this basic Knowledge comes Wisdom and Understanding.

2. We must build our own society; we must have a Culture of our own. Our own crafts, arts, literature, habits, skills, our own way of life.

3. We must learn and practice refinement; One who has been purified, which is to be freed from guilt or the pollution of sin, and attain calm of mind. The wisdom,

knowledge and understanding is passed on to future generations (our children). We must have a general civilization before even Allah can accept and judge us justly. We must learn the basic rules and laws of civilization and then supersede them.

I am reminded of the Messenger's teaching on how Musa had to go into the caves and hillsides of Europe to teach the devil some of his forgotten tricknology. Musa had to look and act savage just like them in order to get close enough to teach them. He had to get them to incline to him (accept him), make friends with them before he could teach them.

If the Honorable Elijah Muhammad had come among us and said to us that we were uncivilized and improperly dressed, most of us would have been insulted. He knew this and used wisdom by coming to us as our friend like Musa before him had done. We didn't know that this was wrong and required adjustments in order to be accepted and respected by civilized society. We didn't know that the morals of a culture is measured by the condition of its women. So Elijah had to come and teach us self value and self respect. He taught us that education and civilization works together. Education means some kind of branch of knowledge that we are trying to get acquainted with, or to teach it to others who do not know it.

Educate means to teach someone the knowledge of another who displays higher places in knowledge. You cannot civilized some one until you educated them into the knowledge of who they are and what's going on in the world around them, even if they have a Masters Degree; self knowledge is a basic requirement. We must be taught what civil acts and ways are in the society of the righteous.

Today, we see in America a supposedly highly civilized country, people dressing in the most uncivilized style of clothing. It is a terrible disgrace to members of civilized societies to see the indecent and savage manner of dress in which the women in America are displayed. It may as well be a nudist colony. Women and girls are kept on display 24 hours a day. They are considered mere obstacles of sexual lust and desire. Even the former head of this country has been charged with chasing and lusting after women. It has actually affected how the American public trust his judgement; however, if the women were dressed properly in loose fitting, longer garments, it might have been easier for him to rule and serve the people better. We cannot walk around men undressed, and dare them not to look. A civilized woman knows the nature of a man and displays modesty and respect at all times.

The Honorable Elijah Muhammad, I can proudly say, is a civilized man. He has not fail to perform his duty in teaching civilization to his people, through F.O.I. for men and M.G.T & G.C.C. for women.

We are not servants any more. He taught that we are being taking from the rear of civilization and placed on top, where we belong as a righteous society of people. We will be the guides for future generations to come; yet, we must qualify to be an example and gain the respect of other civilized society. However until the so-called Negro women stop parading around in public half nude trying to compete with white women and not caring what others think of her, this will not happen. Could one reason for why we behave the way we do, be that we do not know our higher purpose?

WHY DID GOD MAKE THE WOMAN?

The Woman is a Man's Heaven.

Before we start, we shall first elaborate on why we are starting with the Black Woman when addressing why God made woman. We understand that the predominate mindset makes black or talking of black in any way suspect; therefore, we are going to submit a little science which raises the bar in such a way that transcends white racist thought. For this illustration, we shall use a white man's finding, by the name of Gregor Mendel.

The Law of Dominance:

"If one of a pair of genes is dominant and the other recessive, the recessive trait may appear in an offspring only if both genes of its pair are recessive."

In other words, you can get all colors from two Black people, even albino, but two white people can only produce another white person - no more, no less. BLACKS HAD TO BE ORIGINAL! Therefore, the origin of all women started with the Black woman; yet, she was made also, and the rest of that story will be told in another book.

What is the origin of the Black woman? Why was it necessary for her to be made? Will these answers tell us what her role and purpose is? For these answers, we would have to go back to the root of her creation.

According to the Honorable Elijah Muhammad, last Messenger of Allah, the first God Created Himself from an atom of life rotating in the darkness for trillions of years. There were no stars, no moon or planets, because they had not been made yet. He was alone in the endless darkness. To overcome that darkness, He created the sun, thereby having light; yet, having made light, He still looked like that which He came out of, which was the blackness of space; yes, that's right, the God is Black.

The Honorable Elijah Muhammad teaches us that no one knows how long it took God to Create Himself, because there was no one else in the darkness with the capability to record His Creation. He was the first, so we don't know of His beginning. One might wonder how is all of this relative to the Black woman. Well, the Messenger teaches us that, "He wanted a different human being than Himself, so He studied Himself. He "made" a woman by studying Himself. I put emphasis on made, because he used himself as the material. Something created is from nothing. That which is produced or made is from something that's created already.

He made a woman secondly so this would solve His problem of a search or waiting trillions of more years for another Man. He made for Himself, from Himself, a Woman. She was made to conquer death through the law of reproduction. She was made to reproduce God. This is why the Blackman and woman is made from the very essence of God. He made her to give Him peace of mind and contentment, heaven. Someone to compliment His creation. Someone to console Him. One that He could continue reproducing Himself from.

God set a standard, from His own creation out of darkness, for all life to rotate as He had to and come out of total darkness. Today, all life comes out of the darkness of its mother's womb, or from some other darkness. There is nothing spooky about this. I watched a special on TV about childbirth; they showed how life begins, what happens when the sperm of the man comes in contact with of the ovum of the woman. It started rotating. The scientists admitted to not knowing why it started rotating, but this is how God created Himself from a life germ turning in the darkness.

The Messenger teaches us that we should know ourselves and the nature of life. The same laws and principles that were here many, many years ago, are the same ones that are here today. This is the natural order of things. They still apply in these modern times. The universal order hasn't changed.

The Honorable Elijah Muhammad teaches us that as we are the direct descendants of the Creator, all other races came from Black people. Even if one wanted to refute Elijah Muhammad, they can't refute biology, chemistry, physics or, as stated at the beginning of this writing, genetics.

The Black woman is naturally beautiful. When you see her, you are looking at natural beauty. When two people are together and are at peace, they are in heaven. What is above the peace of husband and wife, the Messenger asks? He teaches us that the woman is a man's heaven and they should live together in peace and happiness, especially if she chooses him.

After choosing a wife the man should provide a home for her and it is her duty to make it comfortable and beautiful. A man has no better heaven than a wife, and if there's no heaven at home, then he doesn't have any, because that's where it begins [not in the sky].

Before marriage they are twins, after marriage they are one. They are a part of each other. The woman MUST always submit and recognize man as the head, that does not include wife beaters, bums, abusers, and lazy Negroes, but God-fearing maintainers, providers and protectors. She is not made to be his equal, because by nature, he cannot submit to her, but if he is not on his post, somebody has to be a man - even if it's temporary. The danger is that many of my sisters have had to be the head so long until it seems that it's their rightful place. This is not so. Our man was killed a long time ago and now that God has come and raised him and us, we must now help him back in his rightful place so that he can earn the respect he's due. The creation was made for the man, because he was here first, but the woman is justified in sharing it with him; the glory of the man is the woman.

The Black woman is the first woman. She's the strongest and the best of women; by nature she has a hard job, because she has to civilize the nation, which is our children.

Christianity, here in America (which is a form of mind control), has completely robbed and spoiled the Black woman. It has made her be other than who she really is. She's been a victim of circumstances. So, before she can become responsible for civilization, she must be re-educated back into the knowledge of self, which is by nature, a righteous Muslim. Afterwards, she will know her place and will be taught the importance of her responsibilities.

She is the one who forms and shapes the Black Nation. It is very important how she eats, thinks and act during pregnancy. She must be peaceful and read and study the teachings of the Honorable Elijah Muhammad, and keep up prayer. The woman is the child's first teacher and she should teach by example, so when her children come forth, they will be educated in a high manner and taught how to rule.

It is equally important how she is handled, because if she's treated unjustly and thrown in the mud, then she will bring forth her children in the mud. If she has no self-worth and low self-esteem, then whatever she feels will be transferred into her unborn children. The black man should treat her as if he wants her to give him happiness and she will bring forth rulers for the new world, because this old world is going out.

The Messenger teaches the woman in Islam to dress to please her husband, because his aim is to get respect for her. When she gets the knowledge of self, she will not seek, in the least way, to attract or tempt men by wearing skimpy, form fitting clothes nor will she wear make-up. There's no need to wear make-up, because she has nothing to hide, what you see is natural beauty.

Our God and Saviour, Master Fard Muhammad, came among us and raised up the most Honorable Elijah Muhammad, His last and greatest Messenger, to teach us how to excel all nations: which means: to be better or greater than, by making a law and guide for us, within a special class called The Muslim Girl Training and General Civilization Class (M.G.T. and G.C.C.). This special class will equip us with the necessary qualifications we need to be put on top of civilization as Black women.

THE WOMAN IS THE PRIME FACTOR

I am grateful to be a part of this work of restoration of this mighty black nation and to its rightful place. We as black women in Islam, must work together to become fit for a life in a society away from this wicked one. We must learn these things for they are for our own good.

It is no doubt that Islam is mathematics and mathematics is Islam. Do you know what a prime factor is? As one of my teachers, sister Captain Bayyinah Sharrieff Hamzah said years ago, "We are the prime factor of how our whole nation is judged.

The women, we are the prime factor of this whole restoration of our nation. The prime factor in mathematics is that number by which every other number of an equation or mathematical grouping is divided or evaluated. It is a basic number that cannot be divided itself in practical terms. We are that factor. We are the elements by which our whole black nation is being judged.

When one wants to see the quality or the work of a people, one looks to the woman, to you and me, and by this standard of evaluation, our black nation is judged. We are the ones who forms and shapes us as babies, gives the first lesson to the child and raises and cultivates this child into adulthood.; this is a very important job; it is not an easy responsibility; this is in actuality, God's work, to shape and make a person. This is God's work to help cultivate a mind and to help nourish and raise it.

This society that we live in has made it very difficult to raise a child. In this society, we are ashamed to say that we are a house wife, a home maker or a mother when we're asked about our occupation. This women's liberation group has made the term, motherhood, homemaker, or housewife degrading. We don't want to be regarded as a housewife or a homemaker, or a mother and yet these are very important jobs, our whole nation depends on how well we do this job. Our jobs carries a lot of responsibility. People's lives are at stake with our jobs; the future of our nation is our job, and we are in bad shape.

If we only knew how much the God and His Messenger cared about us, and how much they worked to teach the value of the woman us. How fortunate are we to be the chosen people above all the other nations of the earth; chosen by Allah, Himself to be the first to receive supreme wisdom, knowledge and understanding

The Messengers teaches us that Allah is only after us to make us an example for the world to be guided by. We have been given the tops of divine wisdom and He (Allah) wants to make us into the greatest of all of the people of the earth.

To do this, Allah Himself set up a special class for the training of you and I, the MGT and GCC: the Muslim Girl's Training and General Civilization Class. This class deals with the very basic of what you must know about self to develop self to its fullest potential. This class concentrates on what your duties are in respect to self and other people. Another main purpose of this class is to instruct you in how to act and live in a decent righteous society. It is to teach you those qualities needed to develop your character into a respectful righteous person who can travel the world over and be respected by all who look upon you.

This American society is not for our good; it has never been for our good. We were brought over here from our own land by white America 400 plus years ago not for our good but for their good. We know our history; we know how we were stripped of all decency and self respect and above all the knowledge of our self. We didn't even know our real names. All we know is that we came from somewhere the white man called Africa. We have always been abused and misused by white America. Our fore parent were raped constantly by white America, yet today some of us want to openly give ourselves to white America. We have been raped by them so much that we give ourselves as if it is the norm of things. We even look to them as our example as a woman ; the Messenger teaches us not to use them as our guide even to the smallest things like how to cook, dress, or live.

The Messenger teaches us that we are Muslims by nature (which is a righteous person), the first letter of our class, and the world we are being prepared for is a righteous world, a society of good, and we should work with ourselves to qualify to be accepted by a righteous society.

Many of us may not feel good about ourselves or not pleased with our present appearance as a result of being out of the knowledge of self , living other than the life and not eating the proper food; however, our natural self is the best. We don't need the many cosmetics that the white society has to offer in order to obtain beauty because we are to be made into the most beautiful people even more beautiful than we were before, and all it takes is belief in Allah and acceptance of Him. We must be careful how we dress and wear clothing according to their purpose, that is to cover or body and conceal our form.

If we fear Allah, we will love Him and when we love Allah, we will want to please Him (spiritually). When a woman loves a man, she wants to please him and she is in submission to him, to be shaped by him. This, in itself, is very key and the man should use wisdom by not abusing her or exploiting her submissiveness; that is, if he values his future. Just because he has the muscle and physical strength at his disposal, he must exercise wisdom to build his home in order for there to be peace among the two. They must both respect one another.

The man must be respected for his natural birth right because he we here first, we must honor and submit to him because he is a degree over us; he is of the God by the very nature of being a man. We are from him. He is suppose to be our ruler; we must learn this and he must learn how to rule.

If you fall in love with Allah, you will concentrate your mind and your efforts on cleansing yourself of the unrighteousness that you are practicing and practice righteousness which is the very nature of the original black man and woman; when he can get you the black woman cleansed in the spirit of righteousness, then he will have the original man in righteousness again, because in order for him to produce a nation, the man has to first come to the woman, and if she is in righteousness, then when he comes, then he has to come into righteousness before he can produce more of himself, and from her will come a righteousness nation.

As women in Islam, we must be taught self so we will know self and know other than self. We must be reformed back into ourselves. Until we are careful of what we say and do, we will never be accepted into a righteous society. We must act and become a decent civilized people to get the respect of a decent society or nation. We are what we think. We must clean our selves up and go back to that natural woman that we are by nature.

The Honorable Elijah Muhammad's teachings is to qualify us to go into another world; a world of freedom justice and equality. We must be trained into the knowledge of being a Muslim and practice it. The black woman must be trained into what Muslims look like in Islam. What is required of her in order to be able to compete with the women of the world of Islam. We must be trained and we must master this training. We must be taught how to exceed the Muslim women of the old Muslim world and that God did not come to put us at the rear of civilization, but to put us on top of civilization and this means that we must clean ourselves up to a respectful level, more than any other civilization. This is why we are taught not to style our clothes after this American society.

We must be taught what is necessary for us to qualify to leave this hellish society and enter into the best of civilized society, by becoming a part of the MGT and GCC class."

HOW TO EARN RESPECT FOR YOURSELF

The righteous servant seeks justice to justify his righteousness.

The black woman in America is the most disrespected woman on the planet Earth. She has been used and abused by everyone. She is looked upon as a servant to the world. She has been thrown in the mud. Is there something wrong with her? Why is she being treated so badly? These are very important questions, so let's talk about them.

First of all, let's define respect. Respect means to hold in high regard; show honor or courtesy to, to show consideration for; avoid intruding upon, etc…

What state or condition is the black woman in today? What is required of her to get respect? Where must she go to get what she seeks?

The black woman is in a sad condition, because of the so-called freedom she thinks she has. She has been fooled into thinking that the freedom to come and go as she please, the freedom to attract men by wearing form fitting clothes, the freedom to wear makeup, to compete and look like the white woman, is real freedom.

This so-called freedom causes us to tempt men by any way we can, because we don't believe we can get one any other way other than exposing our private parts like an animal to tempt the animal in men. Consequently, we have reduced ourselves or allowed ourselves to be used as the world's doormat, to be misused and exploited. This is our condition.

The white woman is naturally ugly, with no form, and colorless; consequently, makeup was made for her. False pads, implants and a whole host of gadgets was made so should could be attractive. But you, black woman, God gave you all these things naturally.

As a result of years of unconscious programming and negative image conditioning, the white man has made us, the black woman, believe that we are not only uglier than his woman, but the ugliest woman on earth. Many of us are not conscious that we feel that way, we just automatically act it out.

What does the Black woman need to do to get respect?

The first lesson to the black woman is to respect herself. You cannot expect others to respect you if you don't respect yourself. Stop showing off your forms to everyone and anyone.
Some sisters - yes sisters, I am not concern with what the women of other races does. I am only concern with my black sisters here in America. You make it extremely difficult for brothers to respect you, by wearing clothes so tight, that it looks as if you needed oil to get in them. Then, when you hear the news, you wonder why the rape rate in America is so high. Tell me how many Muslim women do you hear about getting raped or abused.

The Honorable Elijah Muhammad teaches us that the black woman's body should be covered under loose fitting garments. Her beauty if for her husband only. The Messenger teaches us that the Black woman does not need to wear makeup, because she already has plenty of color in her skin. It is the white woman who needs it, because she is of a made race of people. She needs it to keep her made up.

All the black woman has to do is wash her face, keep it clean and eat the way he teaches us to eat, and she will grow into natural beauty, all without makeup. Messenger Elijah Muhammad teaches us that we are seeking the respect of nations. You may ask: where can I go to learn about these things?

Honor, respect and protection that is due The black woman will come when she accept her own and be herself. This is the first and foremost teachings of our Saviour, Master Fard Muhammad, Who had also designed a class for us.

That class is called Muslim Girls Training and General Civilization Class (M.G.T./G.C.C.). It is a class of a high order. To learn the basic rules and laws of civilization, and then supersede them, is a high order that requires a high class. M.G.T./G.C.C.

Can you qualify? It will educate you into the knowledge of a peaceful and progressive domestic life for you and your family.

We are living in the last days sisters. Time is running out for the black man and woman in America. He must get himself together and take his place as ruler, before she can take her place beside him.

WHERE MUST SHE GO TO GET WHAT SHE SEEKS?

This question is best answered by first knowing where we came from and the purpose for which we were made.

In the creator's creation, there is a place for everything and everything is only justified in it's place. If we are to justify our value, we must me in harmony with the reason we were made.

When one reads the story of Adam and Eve in the Bible, many of us walk away thinking that the woman possibly is naturally evil and was the cause of Adam getting kicked out of the garden. The story depicts Eve being approached by a talking serpent and consequently being beguiled into seducing Adam to disobey God. Well, my sisters, this laid a H_ _ _ of a rap on women that still influences how men still treats us until this very day. Yet, the truth has been brought to us and just like it said in the Bible as well, in the book of St. John, 8:32, "And ye shall know the truth, and the truth shall make you free."

The truth of which Jesus spoke was the truth given to us from God. As promised, God has come and raised up the last one, of whom the world had been expecting. He interpreted the illustration of Adam and Eve as the beginning of a new race on our planet, not an actual encounter of a man, woman and a talking reptile. Adam represents the beginning of the white race and Eve is the weaker part of Adam giving in to the Tree with a knowledge of good and evil (or a firmly rooted institution with the knowledge of good and evil). This father or founder (by one man sin entered into the earth - see Romans), a new way of thinking began along with a new people exporting and perpetuating it. It is this frame of mind taken all over the planet by the white race and they have conquered the darker peoples of the earth with it and today we all are victims of this deception.

Therefore, black woman, if you want to know were to go to get the peace of mind, respect, relevance, value, integrity and satisfaction you need, then you must find your way out of the deception perpetrated on you from the slave-master and destroyer of you. The Creator did a good job at supplying you with your needs and have not failed in His promise, don't you think he has the power to restore you?

God has set up a special class for you, but you are caught in between seeking your enemies approval, who have always stripped you butt naked and beastially done everything to you possible or God's approval, Who has now arrived and have shown you nothing but love.

To aid in showing you proof of how we were experimented on during chattel slavery, in the upcoming chapters, we will point it out to you.

ISLAM DIGNIFIES

Islam is the circle of peace and the diameter of happiness.

Islam as taught by the Honorable Elijah Muhammad, is the only life giving teaching for the Black Woman in America. Not only does she learn about self, but also a thorough knowledge of others. Islam teaches the woman her place, purpose, mannerisms and more. She learns that the Black woman is the Mother of Civilization; the best and strongest, because of all women, she was here first and all other women came from her. She is the Mother of Civilization or prime example, the standard from which all other women are designed.

A prime example is different from the common woman; she is honored and respected in a high manner. She is guarded and protected around the clock, and her guards will risk their lives to save hers. When her offspring is brought forth, it is also protected and raised in a high manner and taught how to rule. The same should be for the Black woman. She should be put on a high pedestal as to elevate her self esteem, self worth and to promote the proper raising of here offspring; yet, she is not to be worshipped. Only Allah

God Who made her is to be worshipped. The white race has institutionalized the worship of his women. Notice in his movies. When one man wants to extort another, he kidnaps the white woman, for whom he seems to be willing to give up everything for her. Likewise, in his game of chess, he gives the queen great power. He as well has raised us on his literature with the damsel always being in distress and in need of being saved. Yet, he is the biggest exploiter of his women. They just got the right to vote a few days ago and he has been selling them as much, if not more, than they have been selling themselves. He and the dog have been protecting them since the cave days. It is a mistake to say that dog is man's best friend. The dog is MANKIND'S best friend, and a closer friend to mankind's woman.

Islam teaches us that since the Black Woman is the First of all women, by nature, she has a hard job, because she has the task of civilizing the Black Nation. The Messenger teaches us that Christianity has totally robbed the Black woman of the knowledge of self; so, before she can be allow to teach and train others, she must be re-educated into self. She then will know her place and will be taught the importance of the home and family life.

Islam teaches the black woman to dress with dignity and respect by not wearing form fitting clothes. Not only does this gain her respect, but it also protects her. The American woman wears skimpy, short, see-though clothes and they are raped daily. How many Black women, Muslim followers of the Honorable Elijah Muhammad, you hear of that was attacked or raped? You cannot be protected and respected until you respect yourself.

Islam teaches us to love, honor and respect our husbands as being the head of the household; depend on him, it will give him strength. A great number of us came from single parents, (women most of the time) and we are afraid to depend on the black man, because he didn't know how to maintain, provide and protect his family, but Sisters, it is time for the Black man to rule. We must be understanding and give him a chance by not be an obstacle in his path.

Islam teaches us how important it is to humble ourselves, yet also to be firm, because we may have to stand in and make very important decisions when our husbands are away; however, when he returns, he should not have to ask for his seat back. If he does, that means that you are out of place. Some of us have changed roles so much that we are the mother, father, advisor and business manager. It is difficult for the man to have a soft wife when she is out on front street trying to lead him.

Islam teaches us not to nag our husbands, but find a quiet spot and talk out our differences. We understand that none of us are perfect and we do have misunderstandings sometimes, but the man should not have to raise his voice to control the woman. They both should talk in a very private civilized manner.

Islam teaches us not to be critical of others, but work on self and clean up our bad habits. Sisters, if you see something in another sister that is unpleasant to you, don't get with others and talk about her, but be a friend and help her to help herself by being a good example; she will remember and respect you for it.

Most of all, Islam teaches us not to be envious and jealous of each other, because it is like a cancer; it destroys from the inside out. You will never be happy with self, because you are busy watching the other sister to see if she is prospering. Every thing she acquires, you'll feel as if it should be you.

The only happiness you'll get, is her downfall, and that is not the way of a Muslim Sister. We should want for our brothers and sisters that which we want for ourselves and be happy to see him or her succeed and progress.

Islam as taught by the Honorable Elijah Muhammad will give you a new out look on life. It will put you on top of civilization and force other nations to respect you as a civilized people.

THE IMPORTANCE OF FAMILY UNITY AND OBEDIENCE

We want to make a new nation. Get that in your mind.

When the Messenger accepted the mission of bringing the dead back to life, and giving sight to the blind, I believe he knew that he, as well as his family would have to make many sacrifices, and that his wife would have to be very understanding. According to some articles I read, she was a very strong example not only for her family, but for other brothers and sisters.

Sister Clara Muhammad was the first of the family to accept the mission of The Honorable Elijah Muhammad. She held the Muhammad family together all the while he was on the run. And, while he was in prison, the remaining officials would seek information from her. She would bring understanding from the Messenger on questions she could not answer. She gathered and sent or brought to the Messenger whatever literature the prison would permit.

When the Messenger was incarcerated, Sister Clara followed the instructions he gave her (one mind in unity); she tried to help carry on the Messenger's work in whatever way she could, which is what I believe gave her success in controlling her children. She submitted to his authority and obeyed. Just think if she had not obeyed, our condition probably would be worst than it is today. She was the first example for the black woman in Islam. I have heard many brothers say, "If I am going to follow in the Messenger's footsteps, I expect to have some of the same problems he had." The same goes for us my sisters. If we are going to be wives of men who follow in the Messenger's footsteps, we should expect to have some of the problems Sister Clara had. So let us learn from her experiences.

If the husband is taken away or have to leave the home for long periods of times, the wife should guard his inspirations and protect his interest. That is, she should still carry out his instructions. She should think as he would think: one mind (not on an emotional level; for the devil preys on the black woman's emotions). Here are some pointers to remember. They may even save your family:

(1) Teach the children of Allah and the Messenger, as the Messenger said, "*burn it in their hearts*." (spiritually)

(2) Teach them to obey the Restrictive Laws at home as well as in the Temple, because Islam is a way of life not a religion and the Restrictive Laws shouldn't stop at the door steps of the Temple when we leave to go home.

(3) Teach the family to be understanding and flexible, because sometimes circumstances force their father to make a decision on the spur of a moment. Don't allow them to question his authority, even if there are older children, you are his other half, to question his authority will lead to disobedience.

(4) Teach them to honor and respect the father as being the head of the household and to trust his judgement in making decisions for the entire family, because he has their interest at heart and is trying to prepare them for a world that they have not known.

(5) Teach them to love and respect one another as brothers and sisters.

(6) Never cry in front of the children especially the males, even if you have to hide it, because this will make them weak for they are our future rulers; be strong, yet gentle and if you still want to cry, do it in private (because we are the emotional side of our mates).

(7) Teach them about the importance of having culture and refinement, to pool their resources, (for example, to save money).
Five to six Mexican families will share a 3 or 4 bedroom apartment and within one year, they would have purchased a home for all 6 families). We should learn from the success stories of others. Teach them the price of truth.
Heaven is not something that is given to us, we must earn it. The Messenger teaches us that the unity of our people is the answer to our salvation; unity is the key to success and we must come together in order to achieve the benefits. If we are going to promote unity, a good place to start is in our own home. This is how palaces and empires are built and passed down from generation to generation. We must plant the seed in our children's mind that one day they are going to be great men and women in high places (rulers).

THE BLACK WOMAN'S ROLE IN SAVING OUR FUTURE

As responsible parents, we must properly educate and care for our children. We owe them a living until they are old enough and able to care for themselves. It is our duty to prepare them for a world they have yet seen. This includes protecting them from a world that is full of sport and play.

Sport here is defined as anything that leaves the child idle. When we think of sport, we think of a ball or some game; however, as a people, we were never educated in the higher values of life. Consequently, we are not teaching them to our children. Sport represents a waste of time. God did not create us to wander aimlessly. We are created with a purpose; unfortunately, our slave-masters hid our God given purpose from us, and as the object of slavery, we were only allowed to act out whatever slave purpose he had for us. In fact, we were brought here in America for only one purpose: slavery. We were not ordinary slaves, like one would read about in ancient times; when after a debt is paid the slave is freed. Other kinds of slavery were indentured servitude, in that your family was indebted and it had to be worked off; however, after the debt was paid, you went free.

American slavery, on the other hand, consisted of actually being deprived of the right to know that we were human. We were forced into chattel slavery; thus, putting our parents on the level of all the other livestock the slave-master owned. We were treated in the exact same manner, and many cases worse. The slave-master rarely burned a cow, horse or mule at the stake, or hung them on trees or endlessly raped our women, then sold the offspring of his own loins.

The slave-master couldn't teach higher values, because, as previous cave dwellers, he was borrowing them himself from our ancient fathers, he has been stealing from since being on the planet.

When I say higher values, I mean training our children with an idea of determination. In other words, we as parents must point them in some direction instead of letting them "just" happen into one either from television or their peers who watch television.

The television is the strongest source of subliminal seduction (means of seducing a person by sending messages to their minds without them being consciously aware).

What effect can this world have on a young Muslim sister, who has been privately educated most of her life? What happens if she decides to attend a junior college and is bombarded with a tremendous amount of peer pressure from the other students? Mentally, how will she handle the stress and still be able to achieve an education?

The Messenger stated in the Muslim Program, Want #9 "We want equal education, but separate schools up to sixteen for the boys and eighteen for the girls, on the condition that the girls be sent to women's colleges and universities. We want all Black children to be taught and educated by their own teachers. Under such schooling systems, we believe that we will make a better nation of people. The teachers shall be left free to teach and train their people in the way of righteousness decency and self respect."

If you have no culture, then with what measures do our children use to protect themselves from within one that's hostile. Are they strong enough to withstand the stares and slurs of non-Muslim teachers. Are they strong enough to withstand the persecution and peer-pressure from non-Muslim students, who, by the way, are the majority?

Although many of us are confident that our children are well mannered; however, when confronted by the enemy, will he or she be able to call up what they have learned at home and apply it without hesitation? Well, I am very sorry to say that about 90% of the time, that is not what happens. I have seen whole families go back to the world after letting their children attend the public schooling system.

Let me tell you about some of the situations I went through as an adult in school, as a follower of the Honorable Elijah Muhammad. I attended the city college in Los Angeles. I wore a full official garment to class every day, which consisted of a head piece, rap skirt and walking jacket. There was also another Muslim sister attending the college as well. I told her that I was going to dress as a Muslim in school, and she said she would do the same; however she never did. As a matter of fact, she changed her schedule, but that didn't stop me. I knew Allah was with me; so, I went all the way. A few times, a non-Muslim brother, about 6 feet tall, would come up to me and say something negative about Islam, or he would say, "and how are you Miss Islam, and you can have it." Or sometimes the teachers in the class would single me out to ask questions about religion. I also had a Jewish teacher who would always start talking about Minister Farrakhan when ever I walked in the class room; I believe this was done to stir up a "guilt-by-association" air, so he thought.

One day while changing classes, I was going down the hall and as I approached the corner, there stood two of my teachers and guess who they were discussing? You would think they had more important things to talk about. Then there were the students, most of whom wore very revealing clothing and looked at me as if something was wrong with me. The only person who seemed to appreciate the way I dressed was a South African brother. He said most of the women in his country were Muslims.

If I had been a teenager, I don't think I could have walked in all of that hot hell without getting a third degree burn; however, since I was an adult and had the spirit and fear of Allah and His Messenger, the Restrictive Laws and some worldly experience, I was able to survive the heat.

The Messenger's program was instilled in my mind; I was afraid not to think right, do right and act right, because after being given the knowledge of self, I was responsible for my actions. I was a little nervous about being stared at all day by everyone in the beginning, but I soon stop caring about what they thought of me. That is how I felt at that time; I was an adult and proved to myself that I could handle that type of pressure, but what about our children today, who are exposed to this evil? Can they withstand what you or I went through and be able to fight off the temptation of the world?

Our children are in danger while attending public schools and colleges. In the University of Islam, boys and girls were taught separately, but today in public schools, they all are in the same class room and are exposed to many things.

As I said earlier, I witnessed a family loose three of their teenage daughters to the world. The oldest started wearing makeup and form fitting clothes; then the second one and the third left saying that she don't want to marry a Muslim.

One might wonder did the parents see the change in the children before all of this havoc happen and if so, why didn't they do something before it was too late. Or maybe the parents didn't realize what the children were going through? I don't know what the parents saw, but when they came to the Temple, I noticed many changes in the children, especially the sisters, such as:

1. Rudeness to Officials
2. Wearing makeup
3. Flirting with men in the Temple
4. Exposing their hair

Any parent that knows their children, will notice if they take on a new personality.

If our children are exposed to children who are allowed to have boys friends and girl friends, and have no culture of their own, then we may see our daughter flirting with some brother, or our son kissing some sister to whom he's not married.

Exposing our children to the public school system takes away their shyness. We must understand what children are going through in trying to keep up in white society. The majority of their women and girls are half nude and probably gets most of the attention at school. Now lets think like adults and look at this out of the eyes of the young sister in college. What do you suppose happens to her when she sees all of that attention geared towards someone else (and you know most females like a little attention). She may not be as strong as her mother or sister Captain in the Temple, and the peer pressure of thinking that the other uncivilized females are going to take all of the boys, can change her in one day, regardless of who she is hanging out with at "public" school.

What if most of the females at school don't talk to her, for whatever reason, and only males rejects talk to her? Unfortunately they will be able to get closer and closer to her as a result of her feeling rejected and may want to be accepted by someone. Soon she may want to show her hair and sing and dance to gangster rap or whatever. The very same things can happen to our sons.

Our sons, like our daughters, were once average students, but now after attending the public school system they can hardly maintain a C average. Since they are in college with other students, they feel they have the right to date. Whenever you correct them, they say to their parents," Islam is boring and we can't have any fun." By not preparing a place for our children, this is the kind of thinking that will force our people into genocide.

While reading this article, some parents will probably say, "she must be talking about her children, because mine wouldn't do such a thing." That's how most parents feel about their children, which is why they are in danger of loosing them and their future to this society. I am not writing these words just to fill up a page. I am truly concerned about our future generation. We need a school for our children and the Messenger said the teacher should be Muslim. Our goals must be the same.

We may feel that we can teach them ourselves today while they are young, but once they turn seventeen or eighteen, they will want to go to college and compete with other children their age. The question then becomes, will we have a college to which we can send them? If you have young children and want them to have a better life than what you had, now is the time to do something about it. We need to put our pennies together now and do something about it.

Remember the Honorable Elijah Muhammad said that lazy parents cannot raise successful children.

The Dangers of Enemy or Foreign Education

Your children have to be prepared for a future they have not lived.
You must shape you child.
Lazy parents cannot make a child successful.

Although we love and want to protect them, we must give them room to become who they really are and to express themselves. A good example of this is the Natural Order.

I have heard the Messenger say many times that the first law of nature is self preservation. Whether it be man, animal or insect, when its time to reproduce, they will risk their very life to keep self around from one generation to the next. When Allah created the Earth, life came with it (plants, animals, insects etc.,) as if it was one big package, check and balance.

Every thing has a place and a reason for its existence. We may look at programs on television and sometimes it may seem as if nature has been unfair to the poor deer that can't defend themselves against lions, tigers, wolves and the like. Or what about the poor frogs that get swallowed whole by the deadly snakes or the little fish that is eaten by the big fish and it goes on. Is nature showing favoritism to the strong? Our God and Saviour gives justice to all life; the above conditions are necessary for balance. The natural order has equipped them all with a self defense whether its, speed, smell taste or strength; the death of one means life for others. If the lions didn't eat the deer, they would reproduce faster than nature could feed them and they would die or eat food that is for another kind of animal which would cause an imbalance. If the snakes didn't eat the frogs it would be too many in the pond and they would take all of the food from the small fish, which would die as a result of starvation and all of the other life in the sea that feeds on the small fish would die. Every thing has a place and reason for living, nothing is here by chance.

Take for instance how determined that Red Salmon is to swim up stream to lay its eggs; she knows that once she deposit those eggs in a safe place, her reason for living is over, but she sent herself into tomorrow by reproducing, and when they come forth and reach maturity, they will swim up stream too just like their parents before them. None of the above animals have to force their seeds to be like them; they are fed and protected until they are able to do for themselves; yet when it is time for them to go on their own, the adults in most cases will force the young to leave because they automatically know how long it takes to prepare them. If the animal is not ready to leave or can't take care of itself, chances are it will die. In other words, animals obey that which comes natural to them by submitting to the laws and principles of the Earth.

We are suppose the be the most intelligent, sophisticated and civilized life on the planet Earth; the highest form of life, yet sometimes I think we need to take lessons from the animals when it comes to our children.

The Most Honorable Elijah Muhammad left us highly prepared and well educated on the responsibilities of parenthood through the guidance of F.O.I and M.G.T / G.C.C. classes. We were taught very thoroughly on how to properly rear and protect our children.

No stone was left un-turned. Some of us went as far as taking our children out of the public school and instead, use an accredited correspondence school and taught them at home. This afforded the parent the opportunity of checking the material before giving it to the child. Also, the parents could create their own curriculum thereby adding some Islamic studies to the lesson plan (F.O.I. & M.G.T). At this point most parents would feel quite comfortable because they are controlling all that their children eat (mentally &

physically) see, touch and exposed to. But what are some of the side effects of this controlled protection?

What about when these children decide they want to attend colleges and universities, considering we don't have one of our own, did we over protect them from the world? Will they be able to stand the test of time? Will they be able to identify with their own age group and use some of that supreme wisdom and knowledge they were given, or will they turn on their heels and blend in with their surroundings to avoid criticism from other students? Will you recognize the change in them if they are infected? Here are some symptoms to watch for:

a. Do not discuss Islam with their new friends because they fear criticism or being called a Nerd.
b. Won't study Islam unless forced by parents.
c. Want boyfriends and girlfriends (non-Muslim).
Most of their friends are disbelievers in Islam (society's rejects).
Tell parents lies just to be with disbelievers and hypocrites.
Don't think Islam has any value and as a result they feel they are missing something.
Want what the world has to offer, so they began to envy the wicked.

Began to find fault with Islam by blaming the parent for all of their problems.
Disrespectful and disobedient to parents and will not listen to their advice.
Began to take extra clothes to school or wear them under other clothes. Or start wearing baggy clothes to look like home boys and home girls (slang expressions).

There are parents who see some of these changes and are too lazy to investigate. This list may not relate to your children, but if it does, you and they are in danger of becoming extinct, because your child will be promoting and preserving some one else's way of life, thereby ending self. As the old saying goes, "we are not going to fatten up frogs for snakes." Some of our children went to FOI and MGT classes and were fully taught how to qualify to do for self; so if they are not going to promote our way of life it is best to see the symptoms early while they in school or college.

Parents should never take their children for granted because you never know what they will do under peer pressure from other children. Some parents would get the surprise of their lives if they paid an unexpected visit to the school. All of this may seem unimportant to many parents today if their children are babies or very young; however, the day will come when this problem will be staring them in the face.

Let's learn from the animals by qualifying them to do for self, by giving them a strong base as taught by the Messenger, then what's naturally in them will come out. The Honorable Elijah Muhammad said to prepare them for a future they have not lived.

We must try to shape them into the strong men and women that's necessary to carry on and promote our way of life; and that is Islam.

Control And Moderation: The Foundation For Proper Family Planning

You will do and obey that which you love.

We must become aware of the knowledge of self and the time in which we are living. We must know these things whether we agree with them or not. There is much misunderstanding among us when it comes to personal control and family planning.

The woman needs a thorough knowledge of her body, internally as well as externally. Reading as many of the Messengers books carries its own reward, but there are certain things you won't find in the books today. Various lessons came directly from an M.G.T./G.C.C. Class, that's if you were fortunate to have attend an authentic one or were tutored by a qualified MGT who's living the life. At this late date, it is rare you will find this class given.

Many Muslim sisters are lacking in thoroughly knowing about self, and as a result, some of them are having children too frequently. Most married couples want and expect to have children; it is part of marriage.

They may know exactly how many they would like to have, and at what intervals they want to have them; yet, things don't always work out the way they're planned.

The majority of our women understand their role in reproducing the nation, but does that mean every year? Of course, that decision rests between the couple; however, in the Holy Qur'an, it gives us very good guidance as to how we can plan naturally so the body of the woman can be at its best for this sacred task. It teaches that a child should be weaned after two years. This helps us understand that if from the time the child is born its twenty four months, and the weaning process begins, an average of three to six months should elapse before another child is considered - why? Because biologically, birth control measures are already factored in and initiated with the natural nursing of the mother. In other words, as soon as the mother has the baby and begins to breast feed it, her body kicks in certain hormonal triggers, which will prevent her from getting pregnant again until she begins weaning the first child off her breast milk. Of course, she must breast feed and then wean properly or else, pop goes the weasel again (smile).

The body needs time to rest. Brothers and sisters, you can't keep it under stress all of the time and expect to stay in good health. Eventually, an over taxed body could result in poor health of the children, because the mother can't give what she doesn't have.

Some couples justify the lack of control by quoting the Messenger, by saying Allah will provide, even if they have a hundred children. This may be true, but He gave us knowledge in order to separate us from the animals that will only mate according to a certain plan, place and time. The animals even have a form of family planning. We have the option of factoring in if we have the means to maintain and provide for them once we produce them. This all seems logical, unless you still act as though your enemy will forever take care of you by providing you a job.

We must remember what the Messenger said in the Muslim Program, Belief #9: "We do not believe that America will ever be able to furnish enough jobs for her own millions of unemployed, in addition to jobs for the 20,000,000 black people as well."

There is also the possibility of the family growing too large for the husband's employment. Customarily, he takes on a second job, which generally leaves the wife alone the majority of the time to raise the children. This is generally never a good idea, especially if there are males in the family. They need a strong father figure in light of the slave history, the scares we still carry. When the husband returns, he's too tired to spend time with the children, so he sleeps, wake up in time for a little consolation, then he's gone again. In eight or nine months later, he has another reason to work harder and longer hours than before, and it's an on going cycle, simply because, he and his wife weren't educated on how to abstain when necessary.

Some women have a fear of talking to their husbands about abstinence for what ever reason. Maybe they are afraid he will get angry or look at other women, which should not be the case. If he is righteous, and fasting, he should be able to go without a few days. Even dogs are not always at it! It's not like its impossible; if he is a follower of the Honorable Elijah Muhammad, and have the fear of Allah in him. The woman shouldn't worry about such things. This is not said to throw rocks at anyone, but only to point out the need. Allah didn't make the woman just to be under burden the majority of her life. Consolation comes in different forms other than sex.

Brothers, if she is having them too fast, she may become hard to live with. The Messenger said the worst hell is an icy spirit between husband and wife in a home where there is no peace; yet, how can she give him peace if she is unhappy.

Some women have used Islam as an excuse to go back to the world. Some of them felt they were having too many children. Don't tell that lie and say that God made you put on that Luther Vandross CD and celebrate your way into pregnacy - 5 times? Today, most of us are civilized Black Men and Women and we can't blame Allah and the Messenger for our weakness. They taught us to live in moderation.
Women should understand that it's not just on men to be accountable for the size of the family. They are responsible for a portion too and should do their part by knowing their body and when to expect certain changes. In today's society, there are many methods of family planning, but the best one is the natural method and even that won't work if you don't know the cycle and rhythm of yourself.

The best way to do this is for the woman to reflect back on her very first cycle. On an average, most females start their cycle between the ages of 11 and 12. Think back to how long it lasted; for example, 3, 5, or maybe 6 days, is usually the number of days she will have it until the onset of menopause.

When you were old enough to understand what was happening to you, you should have a daily calendar about your body from day to day, and record everything that happens to you. Another important factor to remember is whether it rotates from the first of the month, to the middle, and then to the end of the month. What about the different hormonal changes the body goes through to signal a change?

We should study ourselves. Perhaps you are waiting for the doctor to tell you what to look for. The feed back you get from physicians is based on the information you gave them. You should know more about yourself than the medical industry does. It may be a good idea to talk with other sisters in Islam who are in similar situations as yourself. You will be surprise as how much you can learn from each other.

I realize that if a woman is now breast feeding, she may not notice these changes, nor will she have a cycle; however, that is where knowing how she was before ever having children comes in handy, because most women can't conceive while they are breast feeding on a regular basis. As mentioned before, there is an automatic turn off switch to give the baby a chance to get out of the way [smile]. Conception usually happens when they are trying to wean the child, and according to the Messenger, it should be around 2 years of age.

However, there is a small percentage of women who, no matter how long they nurse the baby, they still conceive. The woman's role is key because it will rest with her in knowing her body. With the man, the key rests with his ability in controlling his lower desires.

Remember, the Honorable Elijah Muhammad said, anyone who does not have a knowledge of self is considered a victim of either amnesia or unconsciousness and is not very competent. Sisters, we love our families and most of us are fantastic wives and mothers, because we have mastered the art of home making by putting on the teachings of the Honorable Elijah Muhammad, Messenger of Allah. But don't forget, you have a responsibility to yourself.

FEED BABIES THE NATURAL WAY

The Holy Qur 'an teaches the woman to stay in the house and rear her children.

In the Bible it teaches of how God would restore our lives. No doubt, we have been under the conditioning, which made us expect that something spooky and supernatural would take place. This is not true. If you have never experienced any power greater than God's power, which is demonstrated to you everyday through nature, and even through your own life, what is more super than that? There is nothing more super than the natural laws interacting in and around you daily.

Our slave-masters lied to us when teaching us about God, because not only did they rob us of the knowledge about our own land, language, culture, and history, but they robbed us of the knowledge of our God, so we wouldn't know how to call on Him. Consequently, we began worshipping them, because that was the only immediate force in our lives we feared the most. Don't forget, we, like the other livestock were property - and still are. Just in case you're saying in your mind, "I am not anyone's property!" What is your name? Is it of Black descent or European? If you are still wearing the slave-master's name, by international law, you still belong to him. Back then and today, nobody really asked you what you thought about it. That should be a clue.

A people that won't treat you right, surely won't feed you right. Based on this fact, we have had to develop a diet out of the worst food known to man. However, in these modern times, habits and the slave-masters economic reality that was developed on the above same fact, keep the free slave still eating out of the horse's trough (corn meal) and the in-trails of swine, calling it soul food. Black people don't own any industry supplying this stench to them making millions, which they had gotten from the plantation. They just call it jobs today.

The Bible teaches that God would come in the last days, and one of the things He would do is resurrect the dead. Of course, we, as our slave-masters taught us, believed that actual, physically dead people would be raised from the grave. This too, is wrong. It means that a people would be elevated or raised from a condition of ignorance about themselves, God, devil and others. The truth from God about their origin, history and place in the world will cause them to rise from a condition or grave of ignorance. He isn't going to do anything magic or spooky. He is only going to give you truth. The "TRUTH" shall set you free. Free from what? Free from your chains of dependence and fear. But, what about the new life we are promised?

The Bible teaches that when He comes, He will give you more life and life abundantly. How? He would give you more life with the same thing He resurrected or restored your life with: TRUTH! He taught you the truth of How To Eat To Live.

Within the knowledge of how to eat to live, it is pointed out to us that the simple foods are better for us and easier on our digestive system than highly seasoned, rich foods. It teaches that eating natural food will give us natural health, restore our beauty and prolong our lives. Yet, it also warns us about how this world commercializes on just about everything, including food, and if we want to live longer, we must follow God's guidance; not something spooky, but God's natural guidance using natural food. The emphasis here is on the word, "NATURAL."

What do we mean when we say something is natural? Webster's dictionary says it means: (1) Present in or produced by nature. (2) Of, relating to, or concerning nature. (3) Conforming to the usual or ordinary course of nature. With all three definitions, notice how it takes you back to nature, the natural order.

I have heard many women voice a desire for natural child birth, because they are afraid of medications that may harm them and their unborn child. The ironic thing, though, is that after the baby is born, the mother neglects to breast feed the baby with her own natural milk. The society in which we live, conditions us to maintain or regain our forms and get back to that plantation (job); consequently, we put our babies on the new milk on the market (soy bean) and baby formula, and considering that the baby has a very delicate tummy, it becomes constipated and sick. God has come and has given us new knowledge to free us of bad and long lasting health problem by just teaching us better.

Some females don't know how to care for babies or their young children. She doesn't know that it should start with her. A mother should eat good wholesome food as taught by God teaching us how to eat to live. Mothers should breast feed her children. Even though a mother may be sick, her milk is better for her baby than a healthy cow's milk. The mother can drink the cow's milk, and her glands will break it down and put it in the right state for the baby's delicate stomach. The milk from a mother's breast is the baby's first food and there are many vitamins and minerals in a mother's milk that will protect the baby even down to a diaper rash, if cared for properly. Also a breast fed baby has a closer bond to it's mother and will love her more than a baby that is fed from a bottle.

If you are a mother for the first time, please be careful with what you feed the infant. They don't know what's right or wrong for them and will over eat if you allow them to. Actually your milk and a little water daily is really all a new born baby needs, until it is about three months olds. If you feed it food too soon, you definitely can expect diarrhea, diaper rash, sickness, crankiness and it will keep you up at night.

Your milk is equipped with all of the nutrients it needs in the beginning. After the child is about three months old, you can feed it some weak bean soup or mashed apples or orange juice, but this still should depend on the health of the child.

Be careful with the rearing of your children. You cannot care for your baby properly if you have to go to a 9 to 5 job everyday, and feed your baby soy bean milk which will shorten its life. It is too rich for its digestive system. Before an infant is born, it feels what the mother feels and eats what she eats. It is very close to its mother; so, once it's born, it is necessary to continue that bond.

Black Women are the strongest and the best of women; well shouldn't they give their babies the best too?.

Within what God has brought us, acts against our children have been done within the hospital without our knowledge. Don't forget, there is a lot of things we didn't know; for example, did you know that this world is now cloning humans? Do you mean you were not sent a letter or announcement. I am just being a bit funny here, but seriously, there is much you don't know. This is why I am telling you that, as a mother, you must keep your eyes on the nurse. When many of us, who have God's knowledge, go to the hospital, we know this world's history; however the nurses of 2002 have a different technique than the ones of 6,000 years ago; it's all in the milk. Believe it or not.

When feeding our children, we must really understand how important it is to the infant (our future generation). We must start with the mother. She should eat the good wholesome food as taught by God in How to Eat to Live. He said that the mother's milk is the all the baby needs when it is first born. Here is the important question: Have we ever thought why is it so important, or have any of us done the research to find out?

When the slave-master had us as slaves, he performed all types of experiments on us; he knows how our bodies work.

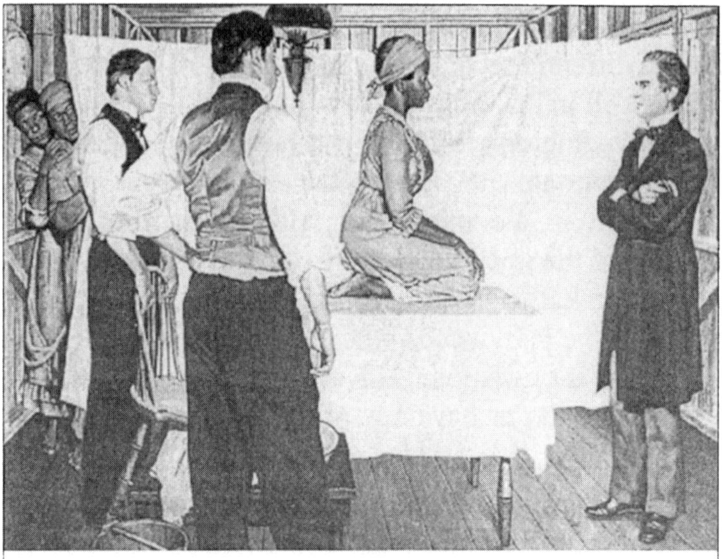

Doctor J. Marion Sims

The Alabama surgeon in 1845 preparing to begin a series of experimental operations on slave women.

MEDICAL EXPERIMENTS USING BLACK SLAVES WITHOUT PAIN RELIEF

Doctor J. Marion Sims,
The Father of Medical Experiments on Female Slaves
The Father of Gynecology

The President of the American Medical Association 1876 and The President of the American Gynecological Association 1876 and The Slave

Women shown in the above picture represent: Anarcha, Betsy, and Lucy.

These three women became the foundation of Sims experiments and the foundation for Women Health.

Anarcha was operated on over 30 times, by Sims. He believed slaves had a high tolerance for pain and required no pain relief from the operations.

Sims Experimented on 11 (eleven) slaves at one time. Black Slaves represented an unlimited supply of people to operate on.

From his experimentation, he was able to determine how many vitamins the milk had in it and how important it is to the child. Remember the slave master had field slaves and house slaves. Well the house slaves ate better food than the field slaves did; so, they were healthier. So when the master's wife had children, she was too proud of her form to nurse her own baby; therefore, the house slave had to nurse it. Now if we were considered to be animals and 3/5 of a human being, why did the slave master's wife force the black woman to nurse her infant? These people had a big plantation with all kinds of farm animals, so you would think that they had more than enough milk, yet she forced the slave to nurse her baby.

We must understand that the devil did not become the god of this world by being stupid; he has studied just about everything he could find, including all types of milk.

Why is the mother's milk so important? What's in it? Many of us would really be surprised today to learn that there are various health conscious groups who agree and practice these things, in order to prolong their lives. For instances, I was reading a magazine from a health food store. As a confirmation of what we knew already from how to eat to live, a mother's milk has profound affects on the metabolism of an infant upon taking it's first drink.

Many health researchers agree that the ideal food for infants is a mother's milk, which contain all the necessary nutrients including water, carbohydrates, fats, protein, vitamins and minerals, to nourish the infant up to the first two years. Mother's milk helps build the child's immune system, assists in normal cellular growth and mental maturation. It also creates a bond between the mother and child. (Soy milk or the cow's milk will not do this.)

Even if the mother pressed the milk from her breast and put it in a bottle, the baby may refuse the milk, because it doesn't feel the closeness of it's mother.

You cannot be a career woman and mother too, this is a full time job.

The Most important time to breast feed is immediately after birth. The first milk (colostrum) is a slightly yellow milk. It is a super concentrated form of nutrients designed to, (1) help the baby nutritionally, (2) act as a laxative to clean out the newborn's gastro-intestional system; and (3) provide healthy bacteria (flora) and antibodies to prepare the baby for digestion of solid foods.

The collostrum will slowly change to breast milk by the third week. During breast feeding, a mother's diet must be healthy. It is important that the mother take care of herself while she is feeding her baby. Studies have shown that vegetarian moms have a lower level of pesticides in their milk than women who eat the standard American diet. There is no substitute for the greatest nutritional gift of all: mother's milk.

Again, most of our young mothers may not be in a Temple to receive the proper training as taught in an MGT and GCC Class, and hopefully this book will help her to understand herself and her child better.

Caring for an infant is a full time job and the milk has given it a natural bond to its mother. Young mothers keep this book so you won't forget the different stages of how the milk will benefit your baby.

REMEMBER ONLY A MOTHER'S BODY WILL PUT THE MILK IN THE RIGHT STATE FOR THE BABY.

HYSTERECTOMY: THE WAY TO DEATH

If you seek to follow wisdom, Allah will help you.

When I think about the many ways the devil tries to cut off the existence of the Black Nation through us, the black women, its not surprising when a hysterectomy is suggested to us as a solution in solving a medical problems. It may sound like a reasonable alternative at the time, but let's talk about life after the surgery. What is the advantages and disadvantages of making this choice?
First of all, what is a Hysterectomy? According to Taber's Medical Dictionary, it means the surgical removal of part or all of the uterus. And the uterus is the organ that houses, nourishes and protects our children from time of implantation to birth. Now let's define it on a universal level.

The Sun is the master germinator of all seeds; it provides light, warmth, heat and the vitamins of life (homornal support, characteristics etc.) for the entire planet earth (the woman, the soil, the body). Well what do you think would happen if one day the Sun suddenly stop operating and disappeared? What would happen to the seeds and vegetation (our children) that depended on it to live and function properly?

Everything would be confused (emotional mood swings),unbalanced (lost of ovaries), non-energetic and fatigued (blood pressure goes up and causes heart to beat faster; thereby, producing hot flashes).

If the real Sun is not present, whose light is the necessary fuel and energy for all life, then moon and star light (artificial estrogen and progesteron) is not the same as estrogen and progesteron produced by the ovaries. Eventually life stops. The planet, (our bodies) will never be the same.

A hysterectomy is a very serious operation. It is the total removal of some parts or all of a woman's reproductive system, such as ovaries, tubes and the womb. What this does is completely upset the balance of her body, in other words, it loses its orientation. If only one ovary is removed, the body may be able to adjust itself, but if both are removed, the body will not be able to control the functions that ovaries are responsible for regulating.

Her blood pressure may shoot up, she may become very sensitive and more emotional than before. She may even feel threaten by other women or she may feel that she is worthless or ugly and that her husband isn't treating her properly and the list goes on. All of this could happen as a result of the hysterectomy; her husband may not have changed at all.

After some women were convinced that it was necessary for them to have the surgery, the doctor has to help them control all of those feelings and emotions by prescribing hormone replacement therapy for the rest of their lives, to protect themselves from the other disadvantages of not having their ovaries, such as Osteoporosis (weakening of the bones).

I have met many black women who have gone through this operation, young, old, single and married, unfortunately most of them felt they didn't have a choice, because the doctor told them it was a matter of life and death. Some of these women were in their early thirties. One of them was in her later fifty's and said to me, "girl, don't you ever have this done to you, because I have never had so many problems." She said she had to take different medicine for nerves, emotions and for proper body functions. She and her husband also separated later. I am not saying it was because of the surgery, but it may have contributed to it. Now she lives with her elderly mother and cares for her. I believe she is very lonely and I feel very sad for her, because its as if her life is over.

I saw a special program on TV that talked about how some complete hysterectomies aren't really necessary, and that you should get a 2nd and 3rdth opinion; even a 4th one if you're not satisfied with the other doctor's diagnosis. I can't speak for other women when it involves making this kind of decision, because it hasn't happened to me; however there are certain guide lines I would try to follow; for instance, (a) I eat as prescribed in How To Eat To Live, as taught by the Messenger (call me for a copy). (b) I fast as often as possible without harming myself, because germs and diseases thrive better in fatty tissue. Also, this would give the body a chance to rid itself of some of the poisons accumulated from previous meals. (c) Breast feeding, according to the Elijah Muhammad, is beneficial for our health as well as our children, (d) Lastly, seek assistance through patience and prayer, because the best cure is the preventive one and Allah already knows what the out come will be.

We must be realistic about our living conditions. We are trapped in a society that drinks and eats poison food and water. It's a wonder we live to get 50 years of age; whereas, when some of us live 70 or 80 years, its a blessing within itself.

According to the Honorable Elijah Muhammad, Messenger of Allah, he and his wife, Sister Clara, knew she had stomach cancer in the early 30's, but she followed How To Eat To Live and it increased her life span until her death in 1972. We can do the same.

Growth, tumors or cancers require a food supply to stay alive; therefore, if we ate the best of foods, as taught by the Messenger, they will fight the diseases that forces us to choose if whether or not we need a hysterectomy.

WHO DOESN'T HAVE A WEIGHT PROBLEM?

The believers will be known, because they will have a mark on them.

Is that new garment you purchased about a month ago feeling a little tight on you? Can't button the neck of your favorite white shirt? If this is happening to you, then it is time to take a serious look at yourself. It could be a health problem, or maybe you need to watch your calorie intake. In any case, you should find out the cause of the problem before you apply a solution.

If you are watching your calorie intake and constantly gaining weight, then you should seek the advice of a physician, it could be a serious illness; however, if you are not watching your calories and eating what ever you desire, it may be difficult for you to determine what the problem may be.

If you want to loose a couple pounds, the first step is to control your eating habits by eating your food slowly and chewing it thoroughly. Take smaller portions and don't go back for seconds, regardless of how bad you want it. Do not try to lose weight too fast. As a matter of fact, you should avoid crash diets. A few people have either gotten sick or suddenly died from crash diets. There is also the danger of developing kidney stones, disturbing psychological changes, and other complications while following such diets.

According to Earl Mindel, some people will go to great length to loose weight, even if they have to induce vomiting or use laxatives. Frequent vomiting and purging can cause chemical imbalances, which can lead to irregular heartbeats and even death.

Dieting and exercising is very hard work, and I believe that it is safe to say that a lot people dread this task, and many give up before they reach their desired goal; therefore, they become overweight and obese (very fat).

As you get older, your body can't break down food as quick as when you were a youth. You tend to not be as active; therefore, it may be best to adjust with your body.

If you have tried the everybody's weight loss program and it failed you, why not try the program of God, in the book, How To Eat To Live, written by the Messenger of Allah (God), Elijah Muhammad. The way the Messenger teaches us to eat is not a weight loss program, but you will not have to worry about dieting or over eating.

He teaches us that by skipping meals and allowing our stomach to rest, we would get beneficial results. I decided to try eating every 48 hours for a couple months and I got amazing results. I just followed the instructions in How To Eat To Live. I still had my morning cup of coffee and sometimes I had a cup of herbal tea at bedtime. It was tough getting through the first couple of weeks, but after that it was as if my stomach knew I wasn't supposed to eat until the next day. I felt very light on my feet and couldn't eat much at dinner time.

I am not suggesting that you should eat one meal every 48 hours as I did, only that I wanted to try it, because the Messenger said I would get good results, and I did.

Taking into consideration that we are black people living here in North America, we don't live in our own controlled environment. We still look to the government for food, clothing and shelter. This alone keeps us under stress, and we're prone to take it out on food.

I do believe that if you have a dieting problem and follow the Messenger's way of eating to live, it will not fail you. You will save money, and you won't have to buy those expensive dieting products any longer. Your best friends will not be heart attacks, over active thyroid gland problems, diabetes or high blood pressure. They will be peace, happiness and contentment.

Try the program of Allah (God), Master Fard Muhammad and His Messenger, the Most Honorable Elijah Muhammad, it works when everything else fails.

BASIS OF A SUCCESSFUL MARRIAGE

If you choose a man to be your husband, you should live together in perfect happiness, especially if you chose him.

Since living in America under slavery, we as black women have been forced to serve the slave-master and his children. As a result of this condition, we began looking up to the white woman as our universal standard of womanhood; for we had no other example. We learned how to cook, clean and care for her husband and family, while she relaxed or did whatever she wanted during the leisure time we produced for her. It wasn't that she gave the Black woman a special class on how to do any of this, she just ordered them to do it a particular way, and through punishment and punishment, the Black woman got it right. For a slave, there was no such privilege as trial and error.

To this day, most of us are still doing things the way the slave-master taught us, and we think that it is the right standard. We have fast learned that a people that won't treat you right, won't teach you right.

For years we had to accept her as a standard of beauty, femininity, morals and ethics, because the white man would not let no teacher from our land come in this country and teach us of our own. We eventually developed "our place" by just doing whatever was necessary to stay alive. History is full of examples of us enduring some of the worst crimes humans can inflict on other humans. It has produced what we believe is our place.

For fear of the slave master's torture of our men and boys, we grew protective. We began programming our boys from birth to not upset the master and don't draw attention to themselves. On the flip side of that, we trained out girls to be courageous and help us protect the boys. This practice seemed ok at the time, but the slave-master knew full well what he was doing. He knew that he was cleverly converting the woman into performing the functions of the man, by being the one who would protect the family, do business with master and be the one who the fearful man would push to go to the door when the bill collector came calling. This practice has cleverly relieved the man of being the bread winner in his home till this day.

The Black man's nature tells him he should be responsible for his home, producing provisions, protection and maintenance for his family, but like it was in more blatant times, the American system defeats him; consequently, he appears weak and pitiful, but sisters, what you don't know is your nature will not let you respect a weak man. So, here we are, both are ignorant to the forces around them that were designed to destroy the black family before it's ever made. Sisters, you say you want a man, but are you willing to give up a power you have been enjoying, that the white man has cleverly robbed from your man? If you want a successful marriage you will have to do so.

Many of my sisters who hear a little bit of this think they can now run off and attempt implementing what they read here. You will be making a grave mistake. If you could have simply read a page and then became successful overnight, it would have been done already. Just as it took time to condition you and the man, likewise, it will take time to de-program the self-defeating condition, then give you the information so you can produce a better condition for yourself. For a condition to elevate you to a higher level, you need a high class.

Marriage is defined, according to Webster II, Riverside College Dictionary, as "the legal union of a man and woman as husband and wife." This union based on a contract. Why most marriages fail is because the two people are not "ONE" on much of anything. Their values vary and when it comes to the higher values of life, for example, what are the children going to be raised as? How will they be groomed, if at all. Most of the time, we send them back to our enemies and expect them to come out right. When our enemies make more willing slaves, we act surprised. These same slaves grow up and do the same thing their parents did. Most people don't get married to expand the higher values of life, because no one teaches them what they are.

When we marry to perpetuate ourselves into the future, producing children to carry the ideals of our family into the future, that's a higher value. When we raise our sons and daughters to improve on business or manufacturing so a better and more advanced family business can be left to the next generation and the next, perpetuating the family name and fortune. This my sisters is a higher value!

The white woman sends her children to charm school or special boarding school or special prep school, because they are grooming them for the future. What do we do, we give ours to head-start. Then we send them to kindergarten and by the time they reach seven years old, they learn how to lie, connive, trick and deceive. Once television is part of the mix, by the time they are 9 and 10 years old, they want a boyfriend or girlfriend, and the rest is history. It all turns into a vicious cycle of self-defeating prophesy.

The scriptures teaches us that in the last days God would come to seek and to save that which is lost, and we can find no other persons fitting this description in these last days more that the American Blackman and woman who are lost from the knowledge of themselves and everyone else.

This is one of the main reasons our God has designed a class for Black women called Muslim Girls Training and General Civilization Class. This class orientates us back into who we really are and what we should be doing. Once the Black woman become a part of the class, she first undergoes the process of re-orientation out of the mind of the white woman and then re-educated the knowledge of the finer and more dignified side self. She must understand who self is and the importance of loving and doing for self. A higher mind requires a high class.

Some of us may wonder why it is called girl's training. Well, this is something completely new to us. We have never heard of this before, so it has to be taught slowly and circumspectly, as if we are children again. We are very young in the knowledge of God, the universe, ourselves and our open enemies. We must be trained into what we are and how we supposed to look, not like the white woman. Since she has come out of the caves, she is seen by the higher civilized women of the earth as a universal Delilah.

We need a comprehensive training to undo the white woman's way of life, which has been imposed upon us. This is why it is necessary to have the right training before marriage. This class will teach you moral decency and respect for your husband, as well as self. It is very important to learn our place and purpose as a wife and mother.

Coming from under the rule of our open enemy, he stripped us of our natural way of life. We naturally knew these things before the American slave-masters robbed our fore-parents. We naturally carried ourselves according to the nature of the Creator; therefore, it wasn't necessary to re-educate us into it. We submitted to the natural laws and principles that governed the universe.

Now that we are understanding ourselves better, we need to be educated and trained all over again. It's like a lion cub being taken when it was young and raised in a furniture store. Once it is grown and you put it back in the wild, the other lions will kill it instantly, because it would be too weak to defend itself. Likewise, we must learn how and when to do the things that we are supposed to do naturally; the birds, bees and other animals are good examples of how to act; they submit to the natural order of things; they just submit to the Creator, we should do the same.

Therefore what better teacher can we have other than one who knows what God wants for us. In closing, Sisters, most of us don't realize how uncivilized and out of the knowledge of self we actually are. Until we are faced with certain difficulties and can't decide how to handle it, we just don't know. Some of us may think we know and have what's necessary to have a happy marriage, but without this class, you don't know what you're missing; consequently you feel you don't need it. We must understand that in order to live and practice our way of life, which is righteousness, we must stop thinking and acting like slaves. We can only do that if we get a new teacher. What better teacher could be better than God?

WHY SOME BLACK WOMEN FEAR MARRIAGE

When two people are together and are at peace, they are in heaven. What is above the peace of husband and wife?

Having doubts about the man you wanted to marry? Are you afraid that he won't be able to support you and a family? What guidelines are you using to come to a just decision?

The above questions are common. Many couples are unhappy and unfulfilled simply because they may have made a quick decision about getting married, actually in the process of walking down the aisles, yet still don't have the courage to say, "I am sorry, but I don't think we should get married right now, because I am having doubts about your ability to support a family."

This is the challenge to a civilized man who would sit and discuss it intelligently; on the other hand, if its an unlearned man who don't have the knowledge of himself, out of more base or lower incentives, he may put fear in the woman, making her too afraid of him to say no.

I receive many letters from other people who have been affected in positive as well as adverse ways from exposure to parts of the truth. Some of them have names that are so long, you can't write it on one line, however, it doesn't mean anything if the woman, or as some call their shacking partner, queen, doesn't feel secure enough to marry him. Some men will put pressure on her and if she is not saturated with the Messenger's teachings, she will not stand a chance in being able to justify her decision; however, some men are very good at demanding and wanting the respect of a god (possessor of power and force), yet they can't support a family.

Based on the lack of knowledge and proper guidance on how to choose a husband appropriately, many black women fear depending on black men for support. They need the proper education on how to choose a mate, as taught by the Messenger.

One of the many talents I admire about the Honorable Elijah Muhammad is that no matter what type of questions people would ask him, most of the time he would take them back to the natural order of things. For instance, the Sun is the master germinator of all seeds. All life submits and stretches forth its arms for the vitamins and nutritional value of the sun's rays. It hangs high in the sky, giving life and light to 9 planets.

If a planet rotates out of its orbit into the path of another planet, chances are it will be destroyed because it won't be allowed to interfere with another planet. The Sun doesn't ask questions. It will not permit any other body in the solar system to corrupt the system. It has earned and demands the respect of all life that comes into being, which depends on it for an existence. The Sun is the most precious gift of gifts. This is Allah (God's) law and order. In His creation, some life will have to submit to other life to survive.

The same applies to the Black man and woman. The Holy Qur'an and Bible both verifies the fact that men are the maintainers of women, like the sun is to the planets; yet, before they can give him the respect of the Sun, he must do the work of the Sun, which is to maintain, provide, protect and fulfill their vital needs. For any man to walk up today and say, "I got it, you can depend on me now," and the woman agrees without some type of history to back him, it is really asking for too much; especially since she's' been providing for herself and children for the past 400 years while the black man was asleep.

She has become very insecure when it comes to depending on him. Any civilized black man having knowledge, wisdom and understanding, should respect the condition she came out of, by proving to her that she can depending on him with works, not a con game or fear. He should not ask for her hand in marriage if he is not able to care for her. Sometimes we use the need to be consoled as the primary reason to get married. If we do, heaven will be over after the wedding day. Self preservation should kick in as a learning device, to seek knowledge about the person.

To what special class does the Black woman of America have access? What class teaches her how to choose and care for a husband. What class does she have that teaches her on the basis of a standard to choose one? What class teaches her what to check for and how to check? What class teaches here how to conduct some type of background check into his family, friends, etc.... When a couple marries, it is not just their coming together as one, but also the two families are becoming one, so it is best to walk into this marriage with her eyes wide open and both feet on the ground, (meaning be aware of what's she's getting into).

Another factor is to check to see if he is a faithful believer in God. Does he want a family and if so, will he be able to support them? Most of all, she should not rush into a marriage. If she feels that this is not the person she wants to spend the rest of her life with, she should wait, Allah is most merciful and will give her the right mate.

I hope and pray to Allah God, Master Fard Muhammad that the information written will be a benefit to any Black woman seeking guidance. This wasn't done to belittle our men, but rather to help our women. If you are a Black man and feel that these statements are offensive and critical, then, what I said don't apply to you. The Black men I'm talking about are righteous, civilized, hard-working and are not afraid to face responsibility and are ready, willing and able to earn the respect of their woman as the earth respects and revolves around the sun.

Can We Depend On The Black Man?

A man should love his family regardless to whom or what because it is part of himself.

Has the black man been on the run to avoid his responsibilities as a husband and father? Is he lazy and always expecting handouts from others? Does it bother him when his wife goes to the white man for financial support? Where was he when we needed him?

We are taught that a man should love his family regardless to whom or what, and that he should control, maintain, provide and protect that family. If a man cannot control his family then, he should not be put in charge of a nation of people. Many men are judged and respected according to how they care for their family. They need that family to preserve and perpetuate himself.

It troubles me to see how some families are separated and mistreated in various foreign countries. The men are shot and put in mass graves, leaving behind many unprotected women and children who are constantly raped and murdered by their captors. This is why we as black women, must be capable of surviving, because many black men have not been mentally or physically able to maintain, provide and protect us for the last four hundred years. We are aware of how the enemy took a righteous, civilized man and changed him into something other than himself, (which is a righteous Muslim) and put him on the level of a beast. He was stripped of his pride, dignity, self esteem and even the desire to want to do for himself. He was robbed of the knowledge of his duty to self and kind. In short, robbed of his home and family.

I believe there are many black men today who are remorseful and feel apologetic towards black women and children, for the suffering and abuse they had to under go for so many years, while the man was mentally asleep and dead. They can not take back the pain nor the damage done to them. What happened, wasn't entirely their fault.

Coupled with that is the fact the woman is the children's first teacher; therefore, the perpetuation of most of the effects and scars of slavery also fall at our feet. This is to keep down any angelic thoughts.

It was prophesied to Abraham in the Bible (Genesis, 15:13) that his seed shall be a stranger in a land that wasn't theirs and that they would be afflicted and shall serve a people for 400 years. So it is plain to see that the Black man had no control over his destiny. He was a victim of circumstances, and based on that factor, I am confident when I say, we (the black women) forgive you, but now it is time to assume your responsibilities as a ruler of our people and heads of our households. The black man should not have to apologize for what he couldn't do for his Family, four hundred years ago; however, if he is still apologizing and can't fulfill his obligations today, then, one might wonder about the certainty of that repentance.

The Honorable Elijah Muhammad, Last Messenger of Allah, teaches us that the duty of the black man is to do something for his black self and black kind. The duty of the black man is self-preservation. He said that a well educated, cultured and courteous people make a beautiful society when it is spiritual. Good manners come from the civilized man who does not fail to perform his duty.

We are living in the last days and the changing of worlds. We must realize the necessities of life to survive. Black women and children needs civilization, they need their own community, their own educational system; we need to live as a nation of people in order to gain the respect of other nations. We can't acquire the necessities of life without the support our men. Don't apologize anymore, Blackman, just go to work and accept your responsibilities.

WE MUST FORGE A WAY FOR FUTURE GENERATIONS

There is no Nation that can get up unless it has a knowledge of engineering.

When our Saviour, Master Fard Muhammad, came among us, raised the first begotten of the dead, His Messenger, the Honorable Elijah Muhammad, and taught him the knowledge of self and others, many times He would use Himself as an example to make certain points.

According to the Honorable Elijah Muhammad, in 1932, our Saviour allowed Himself to be persecuted, by choosing to suffer 3 1/2 years to show His love for His people who have suffered over 300 years at the hands of a people, who by nature, are evil, wicked and have no good in them. He was persecuted, sent to jail in 1932 and ordered out of Detroit on May 26, 1933. In 1933, He came to Chicago and was arrested almost immediately on His arrival and placed behind prison bars.

Our God and Saviour didn't have to submit to this kind of treatment, but He submitted Himself with all humbleness to his persecutors. Each time he was arrested, He would send for the Messenger, so that he could see and learn the price of truth for us, the so-called American Negroes (members of the Asiatic Nation). He was well able to save Himself from such suffering, but how else was the scripture to be fulfilled? We followed in His footsteps suffering the same persecution.

After the Saviour left our midst, the Messenger rolled up his sleeve and went to work teaching us and allowing himself to be persecuted for the cause of truth. They both taught by example and left guidelines for black people to follow. Those guidelines were given in two classes, FOI and MGT. Some were given by word of mouth and some were written on paper; however, regardless of the form in which they were given, someone was made responsible for passing it on to others.

Looking at the condition of our sisterhood today, one must wonder if the word was passed on to the new generations, or was it kept only among some of the first pupils?

Let's look at the meaning of M.G.T and G.C.C., Moslem Girl's Training and General Civilization Class. Notice that girl's, training and civilization are the three key words. Why? The Messenger teaches us that when we accept Islam, we must be totally re-educated into self and kind (the Christians call it brain-washing). In order to be re-educated, our minds must be cleansed of all impurities imposed upon us by Christianity. We must be taught and dealt with in a unique and skillful way.

Unlike the way the world has dealt with the black women in public schools and colleges, very vulgar and indecent, she must be dealt with in a highly civilized manner. As young girls in this wisdom, there are many things that we are not aware of; therefore, it would be easier to receive, if those who are teachers remember the condition we were in yesterday.

Our training must consist of drilling, teaching and discipline, in order to qualify for a certain standard of civilization, of which Allah and His Messenger would approve. Civilization means, one having knowledge, wisdom, understanding, culture, refinement and is not a savage. Pursuit of happiness.

Definition is very important, because it serves as the basis on which rests very important principles. The obligation rests on the civilized to make sure that the uncivilized get the necessary lessons that would prepared them for today. Contrary to the above, in some circles there is a lot of slack talk, gossip, back-biting and ungrounded condemnation.

The Messenger writes in his book, Message To The Blackman, that good manners comes from the civilized man who does not fail to perform his duty. Some of us have not done our duty; yet, we turn our nose up at the uncivilized person instead of educating them. The answer to the question of why is new generation doesn't have access to the truth as the ones before, is evident. The new question should be: Are we being brain-washed again? Will the new generation have to be subjected to trial and error, hit and miss, bumping their heads in the same spot, falling in the same holes as their parents before, reinventing the wheel? The Messenger said, blessed are those who forge first to bring the way for others.

Christian books, pamphlets, and the like are everywhere; that's how they produced rulers. We should have the same motivation about our sisterhood. I am reminded of how the Messenger teaches about protecting the woman and keeping the enemy away from her. If we have a vegetable crop we will go out and turn the leaves and check for bugs and worms to preserve it. We will go out into the cotton field and look for the enemies of our cotton and try to kill that enemy. We study poisons and chemicals of the earth and we pour these chemicals on the enemies of our crops to keep the enemies from destroying them. Well, isn't it our responsibility to feel the same way about our present sisterhood? Don't they need cultivation and refinement, (leaves of Islam need to be turned up to check for infestation of Christianity), to be prepared to help others grow, to break through the surface, so it will be easier for those yet to come? Or are we getting a little insecure and feel that if we give too much too soon, we will loose control of the people?

If you are in fear, put your work in a book and you won't loose control, but you will live on in your work, and you would have earned some blessings from Allah; this is called culture and refinement.

THE BEST RESTORATION IS DONE BY EXAMPLE

Blessed are those who forge first to bring the way for others.

There are many young Muslims women who have written me in regards to proper dressing attire in the work place. They're confused as to what is appropriate so that they wouldn't violate any principles of beliefs in Islam.

The Muslim woman's base is in the home taking care of the family so teaches the Honorable Elijah Muhammad. He doesn't encourage us to work outside the home but, based on the fall of the black man many years ago, the black woman has been cleverly placed in the bread - winner's position. It is easy to assume that most Muslim women don't work outside the home; however, times are very hard and we don't live in an ideal scenario and if we have to work outside the home, we want to feel comfortable.

It is very easy to pick up a book of rules and regulations and tell a person what they should or shouldn't do. Which is good, we all needs these things to govern ourselves by; yet, there are principles and exceptions to the rule. I know in principle that we should wear full MGT garments in ordinary cases everyday. Yet, if I worked in my own business or a Muslim own business, my clothing would be Muslim attire; however if I worked out in the public, in an office setting for example, I would dress according to my circumstances as long as it doesn't violate my religion. I don't think that is the place to wear my holy robes.

We must use reasoning and common sense. The first question we should ask ourselves is are we wearing the clothing according to their purpose, which is to conceal the form? They should fit loose as not to attract attention to the body. The fashion industry has changed to fit the need of the people. It is very easy to find an intelligent pants suit or ankle length skirt suit and matching scarf. Or if you work in a factory, there are many long loose fitting clothes to choose from. I've work in Corporate America for many years and I had to go through a lot of what they're facing today, so I hope this information will be helpful. A good way to start is use the principles of Islam as well as the rules so you will know when to use what (conditions change).

I have quite a bit of experience in adjusting my wardrobe to fit the present circumstances. I've pricked the curiosity of many Muslim sisters and they have asked a series of questions: Do I design my own clothes? Why don't I have on a rap skirt instead of pleated pantaloons, or that I look like a foreign Muslim, or who are you with and why do I wear a scarf instead of a head piece? Why don't I have on the **ORIGINAL** garment? I am confronted with questions like this periodically.

Some times other sisters tell me how beautiful my garments look and ask will I sew one for them? Yet after presenting them with the garment and they wear it around their old friends, they are critique so much that when they come in contact with me again, they began questioning me as if this is something new to them. This goes back to how to use rules and principles. The Messenger teaches of a new Islam; yet the principles will remain the same. We must keep up with modern times.

Things that happen in the past with the first believers are there as a lesson for us; we must go forward. Some of us really need to take a good look at other believers and ourselves because if we do, we'll see that even though we say we are wearing the **"ORIGINAL"** uniform, none of them are the same. Personally every Temple I visited, the sisters looked different. Some of the garment tops were too short, some were long, some had no collar, some wore head wraps and long princess tops and pants, some had on scarves or head pieces and some were not dress in Muslim clothes at all, and the differences goes on; however, back to my point and that is the majority of them don't look the same; I remember also when I was looking at an old University of Islam Manual, the Messenger's daughter, Ethel was allowed to teach at the University and she was wearing a black outfit with a black thin scarf; so its not like this is something new that the believers started wearing in 1996.

I am not saying these things to justify myself or anyone else because justice will come from Allah; what I am saying is that it is easy for some of us to sit back and be critical of others; yet you see them going to work on the slave master's job, in his court system, hospitals, law firms or postal service and we all know that you have to wear the required uniform to work at most of these establishments. However, these very same people will eat the flesh of a young or new believer for wearing pants and long covering top; when in fact they are nothing but "Sunday Muslims" themselves (meaning, all through the week we look like a non- Muslim, but on Sunday, they are holier than thou, a righteous Muslim.

There is nothing wrong with seeking employment on a job; however, if they can find that kind of justification for themselves, of violating their own dress code in public, surely they can reserve their criticism of a new person who don't know or can't afford any better.

I am not saying this to eat the flesh of my sisters, but only to say that I would rather look like a foreign Muslim any day of the week and still stay within the principles of Islam as taught by the Honorable Elijah Muhammad, than not to look like a Muslim at all.

For the record, how I dress is a compilation of what I learned in the Temple from MGT Captains from around the country. If it is thought that I am in error for submitting and obeying an official, then Allah is the best Knower.

The Honorable Elijah Muhammad teaches us in the Restrictive Laws that Insubordination is forbidden. We should all know that when something is forbidden, it is a sin. So when the Captain said this is how the Messenger wanted us to dress in the last days, I could have taken a position and said, "I don't believe you;" however, since I wasn't there and I don't know what the Messenger said to her, myself as well as many others obeyed. If we have been mislead as a result of obeying our Captain, then I don't believe Allah will punish us for submitting because He knows our intent. Sure, there's always the possibility of being misled, but that falls on the one who willfully misguides those who belong to Allah. He is the Master of the Day of Requittal. There as well maybe other consequences we may have to deal with as a result of obeying those in authority over us.

The uncertainty of the time has made it necessary to consult the recordings of the Messenger, his writings, his officials and good judgement with any instructions to which I submit. We are taught to obey those in authority over us, Muslim and non-Muslim, as long as it doesn't conflict with our religion. I don't encourage a new person to come in the door questioning things they know nothing about. This is why I encourage you to learn the program, what the Messenger teaches, first, then you will know that which conflicts. After you come into the valley of decision, what you do is what you are judged by.

As far as older sisters looking down their nose at how some of us are dressed today, well I don't believe they wear that white MGT uniform in the court - house, when they punch the clock. Also if ALL of the MGT Captains were unified as taught by the Messenger, we would all look the same. Most sisters who are new in Islam don't know what to say when faced with a

Captain who says, "I was in the Nation when the Messenger was here and he personally told me how we should dress and act in the last days, or the Messenger said this or that and you weren't there so you should listen to me," and so on and so forth. If you weren't there, and its not written in the books, you don't know who to believe. Although a picture in a yearbook, newspaper, or previously published brochure, is worth thousands of words, what's not there is why the differentiation over a span of forty - five years. The principle of why they were constructed in various ways at various times is the main thing, the best thing. The original man and woman takes the best part. They don't care about the poor part.

Maybe that's why there is such a big division today. The Messenger said that proudness is a sickness and this is why we are divided. He said we will all be one or nothing. Look at the black woman's condition today, has the prophecy been fulfilled?

Below is an example of different garments worn by sisters in the Nation of Islam. You have the Messenger's wife, Clara Muhammad the two Captains of the Nation.

DISTINGUISHED MUSLIM WOMEN hold timely discussion on dynamic role of the Black woman at Muslim Women's Hour at spacious Salaam Restaurant. Shown at increasingly popular afternoon gathering are (left to right): Sister Captain Mamie 2X McCully, Mosque No. 27, Los Angeles, California; Sister Clara Muhammad, wife of the Honorable Elijah Muhammad, and Sister Bayyinah Sharrieff, M.G.T. Captain.

PREPARE YOURSELVES FOR THE NEW

All the world of Islam has to learn what has happened here in America. Islam of Muhammad of 1400 years ago served that time. We need a new Islam to serve this day. My mission is to convert all black people on Earth into the knowledge of God. Acquaint them all with a new Islam and God. There will be a new world all together.

Why are we taught of a new heaven, a new earth, a new way of life, a new government and a new people? Does that mean we should start preparing for the new now or wait until we can identify it with our five senses (see, hear, smell, feel, taste)?

We are a people living in a world that's about to change. Many of us say we want to go with the new, but our actions indicate that we want to stay with the old. There are those of us who would want to see a new world order come about so we could live in peace and happiness; yet, we won't do what's necessary to bring it into being. When something new is mentioned to us, many of us fear a loss of property, control and then again, we may be satisfied with the old.

What is new? Webster's dictionary gave several good definitions: (1) Never used before. (2) Recently arrived or established. (3) Coming after or taking the place of a previous one or ones. (4) Modern or current. There are many more; however, theses seemed the most befitting for the question I am about to ask. Based on the definitions above, can we assume that the reason the we're being taught of a new world is because something is wrong with the old one, and we should prepare our minds for a new one?

The scriptures say that there will be a new Heaven and Earth. This is defined in physical terms as freedom, justice, equality, money, good homes and friendships in all walks of life. Living under the rule of the slave-master for past 400 years, has made it impossible for the black man and woman to have heaven, like we see the white man and preachers, even though the black woman is the black man's heaven (spiritually).

What we are now finding out, is that the white man was only given enough knowledge to rule for 6,000 years and after that time, the original rulers of righteousness would rule again. The old will be replaced with a new world order. With all of the above in mind, shouldn't we do our part by looking for the new? If we want to progress and transition into the new world, can we do this by looking back at yesterday? We must understand also that living in today's society, certain circumstances have changed since the departure of the Messenger, and we may not be able to use the same method of solving a problem as he did 30, 40, & 50 years ago.

In order to deal with some of the new pressures the slave-master has put on us as a people, we must have a new way of thinking. Many of us try to control our children by saying to them, "that's the way 'we' did it yester-year." Do we really expect that alone to have an impact on that child? We are not taking into consideration how they feel when Thanksgiving, Christmas, July 4th, etc.. comes around, when they see other children celebrating. What do you have to offset the emptiness they feel? What help can you offer them in fighting the feeling of wanting to be a part of it? This is a serious question, especially if you don't have any type of community, culture or alternative.

We aren't thinking wisely about the future of our civilization. We're caught up in our own emotions. Our children look forward to being with other young people their age. When they get older, they begin looking for husbands or wives. This is a function of a community. You can't fight a culture unless you have one. You must fight culture with a culture. Out of a misunderstanding or sheer lack of knowledge, we think that just having them read from books, sheltering and close monitoring, that alone will preserve them. With this shallow veil of cultural dressing, we allow them to go out into the world thinking that this is enough to strengthen them against the powerful culture that's out there already.

We have for so long pointed to sheer knowledge in a book without a practical sample of what we preach. We must be wise, that if we are going to use the others as an example, then we should have enough sense to do it with the practical application that goes with what's in the book; otherwise, we could be charged with lying to the people. One of our main problems is using yesterday's mode of operating, thinking that we are going to produce something new. I have heard it said that the definition of insanity is to continue doing what you have always done, while expecting something different to happen. Sometime we force our children to perpetuate this insanity by making them think that by sticking to unproductive tradition, that it is still progress.

How could we hold a straight face, with no progress, and tell them we are following the example of a producer. To make something new, you must go to the root. To bring about a change, you must change the way you think. Once you learn the nature of a thing, you know what it will or will not do. Shouldn't we be looking for newness in all things (food, clothing and shelter), in the new world? What kind of vegetables will we eat? Will our clothing be as they are today? So many of us can't get past this alone. What kind of currency will we use? What kind of homes will we live in? This may sound far-fetched and futuristic, but we have to think futuristically; otherwise, this world will destroy our distinction.

The scripture teaches that God will make all things new; well, how should we look for that newness if we don't use "new" knowledge, wisdom, understanding to recognize what we are looking at? We must learn to put things in there proper place, so we can go forward to preserve our distinction.

Mere belief won't be strong enough to save them. We must give them a reason to be optimistic, considering we don't have a culture for them. It is difficult to show most children idealism. We must prepare them for the new. If we don't, they will make the same mistakes as the ones before us did.

WHAT HAS ISLAM DONE FOR ME?

Let me tell you briefly what Islam has done for me. As a young adult, I didn't know a thing about Islam until one day I got an urgent phone call informing me that one of my brothers had died. I went to the airport and tried to book a flight as a standby passenger. I had never flown on a plane before; so, I was very nervous, and I was upset about my brother. Of course, being young and out of the knowledge of self, my favorite clothing was designer jeans and high heel shoes.

As I waited, I noticed 2 black men from across the room talking to each other and looking me up and down. Then further down from them, there was another young man, very clean and neat. I noticed he was reading a book and he never looked up until it was time board the plane. (How did I know he never looked up – right?)

Since I was a stand-by passenger, I had to wait to see if there would be any vacant seats. Finally the stewardess came for me and as we boarded, I saw a vacant seat between the two men I tried to ignore in the airport. They looked as if they were about to flip the coin. But all praises are do to Allah, Master Fard Muhammad, because to my surprise, there was another vacant between a teenage Caucasian and the neat young Black man that was reading in the lobby. The stewardess directed me to sit next to him. Oh, by the way, the book he was reading was a Holy Qur'an.

As I stated earlier, I had never flown on a plane before; therefore, I was very nervous. So, I started a conversation with the brother. I noticed he was different, because he allowed me to speak first. However, when he did speak, he taught me the whole trip. He reached his destination before me, so he gave me a temple business card.

After returning to where I had initially departed, I attended the temple where he went and became a part. I was very independent and had many personal problems; this brother virtually solved all of them. I was so grateful, I married him.

He took me out of the work place and created a job for me by showing me how to use my professional skills to benefit self. He encouraged me to make my own cloths, brought books and other material for me to study. He took me around the country in the company of many of the Messenger's top laborers, this educated and elevated me, and made me well rounded.

He introduced me to HIGH CULTURE, took me to the finest hotels, made it possible for me to be trained by some of the Messenger's BEST SISTER CAPTAINS and produced an atmosphere that is making me exactly what the Honorable Elijah Muhammad said I am, THE BEST.

So today, when my husband, Minister Nasir Hakim, writes or speaks, please read or listen very closely to him my sisters, he will tell what the Messenger said of our Saviour, Who was born for you and I.

He did not meet the Saviour, but Elijah Muhammad, the Messenger of Allah, did. My husband is His Minister. He will do for you what he is doing for us. The Minister has taken the MEDICINE OF TRUTH, which Jesus said would make us free. This truth from God Himself, given to The Honorable Elijah Muhammad, has made the Minister a teacher, not an abuser; a personal enhancer, not a physical abuser; an elevator of persons, not a mistreater. I am a living example. I now understand my role and my responsibilities, this place is where lies my value.

He is a true counselor, a true friend, and a true Minister of the Honorable Elijah Muhammad.

THE BLACK WOMAN DESERVES THE BEST

My sisters, don't you want to be the best? Don't you want to be in your place of not being looked down on as gutter trash, sex toys and prostitutes? Don't you want to be part of a class that elevates and raises you high? Then to be raised high you must be part of a high class. This class was designed by God Himself to raise you high and put you back in the high place you once were. The M.G.T & G.C.C. is that class. If you are interested in being a part of this class, please contact me and I will tell you how.

Thank you my sisters, and you too my brothers for reading these words, as I close in the way that I opened, which is in the Name of Almighty Allah, Master Fard Muhammad and in the name of His Last and Greatest Messenger, Elijah Muhammad, As-Salaam-Alaikum.

INDEX

THANK YOU FOR PURCHASING THIS BOOK. WE TRUST THE READING WAS REWARDING AND ENLIGHTENING.

We offer various titles by Rose Hakim, as well a comprehensive collection of Messenger Elijah Muhammad's works. These works include:

- Standard Published Titles
- Unpublished & Diligently Transcribed Compilations
- Audio Cassettes
- Video Cassettes
- Audio CD's
- DVD's
- Rare Articles
- Year Books
- Annual Brochures

You are welcomed to sample a catalog of these items by simply requesting a FREE archive Catalog.

Our contact information is as follows: